MY GOOD

A new day has dawn and the spirit is tired; not relaxed.

I don't think it's confusion; just had a bad evening and a bad so far this morning.

Holiday season is gearing up and instead of my continued peace and tranquility; I get noise and people showing up at my home unannounced. Yes this is annoying as hell; thus 2016 I have to put a full stoppage to it when it comes to my second child's friends.

2016 must see him going to their house; his friends' home and annoying their parents with the noise and late stay. I can no longer pay rent for him and his friends. I need a break from them; thus I have to do all to move thousands of miles away from them to a place where I know they will not come. Siberia is looking great but the cold would and will kill me. But if I could move to Siberia and manage the cold; I would just to not have them come to my home so often.

It's funny my son rarely go to their house and some, he can't go to their house; so why does he constantly allow his friends to come to my home and stress me out. Yes I asked him this question and he said, "mom I don't invite them here, they just come." Yeah right with him. Thus I tell you, when you are trying to be clean your children are the ones to break you down with some of the friends they keep. And don't go there because each of my son's friends are characterized and or put in a bracket by me; thus I know the Judas in his life and he doesn't know it. Well I told him, but he just toss things to the side as usual. Teaching black children the truth is freaking hard you know. **_Eee cum eene like tic pap inna dem heaze ole an lodge dey fi dem nuh listen._**

Laade have mercy Lovey; mi si yu plight to yass when eee cum eene to fiwi own.

Wi dyam dunkcya. Anna wen di debil a beat up pan wi haade; das when wi a comea running to you fi help.

Auta yu tell wi nuh fi du wrong wi nuh listen; an now wen wi a get batta bruise wi a cry to yu. Fi wa?

Wey wi a cry to yu fa?

We were the ones to not listen.

Yu tell wi nuh guh desso wi guh desso.

Yu tell wi nuh let evil men into wi garden; wi let dem (evil and unclean men) eene. Eve

Yu tell wi nuh goh inna di way an pathway a di wicked an evil, an wi goh. Psalms One

Yu tell wi sey wi fi kip wiself clean, an wi nuh listen.
Yu tell wi sey fi nuh cheat pan yu, an wi nuh listen.

Wi cheat pan yu with other gods; thus disobeying the <u>"thou shalt not have any other god before me"</u> law as written in man's nasty and unholy book called the holy bible.

<u>And people, the "thou shalt not have any other god before me" is a true law. Therefore, I am confirming this law in goodness and in truth.</u> **You must adhere to this law of cleanliness and truth. You cannot cheat on Lovey and if you are cheating you have to stop and stop now. You are duly warned.**

Brutality comes when we disobey Lovey and trust me; I know for a fact that none of you can bear this pain. I did not listen to Lovey due to lack of knowledge and I felt the pain; severe pain. <u>So it matters not if we know or not. When we disobey the commandments and laws of Lovey, death comes with pain.</u> We feel it (severe pain) for days months and years before death takes you. We were told, <u>"the wages of sin is death."</u> Therefore and thus, this law is true also and I am confirming this law. Because of sin we see death. No, billions of you cannot see death nor do you know what death look like. But from these books you know what death looks like and how death comes. You know the truth of life and death, so live your life to the fullest, but live it (your life) true and clean not dirty and or filthy. And no, religion is not true life; nor can religion get you in the good and true abode of Lovey.

Religion is death thus man kill for religion; death. We destroy and kill; thus disobeying the "thou shalt not kill" law.

If religion was so clean, why is death associated with it; religion?

If religion was so clean, why are the members that are associated with religion so dirty and filthy; unclean?

If religion was so clean, why are the members that is associated with religion not telling the truth?

Why do they, including you break every law and or commandment of God; Lovey?

If religion was so clean and pure and of Lovey, why are filthy and dirty people in churches (your churches of whoredom and sin) professing to be worshipping and praising Lovey when you are truly not?

If religion was so clean and pure; holy, why are you the members associate with religion so disrespectful to Lovey?

If religion was so clean and pure; holy, why is religion so dirty and unclean?

If religion was so clean and pure; holy, why is everything that is filthy and unclean associated with all facets of religion?

<u>You say religion can save you and religion is clean and holy, but yet you keep the his home; the home that you say you've given to God; Lovey, defiled and dirty; sinful.</u>

All this and more is done in your so called churches, temples, mosques, synagogues, shrines and what have you. So tell me, **why should Lovey look to any one of you and give you a saving grace?** *And don't you dare tell me we have sinned and are short of his glory. You know you've sinned so repent of your sins to him (Lovey) and with him (Lovey) come on now. If you truly love him (Lovey) and want a saving grace for self, others, your land and community including this earth and universe, clean yourself up and repent of your sins so that you can and will be saved. I've told you, Lovey doesn't lock anyone out of his kingdom and abode. We are the ones to lock ourselves out due to our sins.*

Strayed

I don't know what to do so I am going to interrupt the flow of this book yet again. This dream I had just now is nagging me. I had two but I can't remember the second one fully, but this one; my first dream won't leave me.

Dreamt this light skinned young black man. He's not too tall and he had beautiful light skinned. He wore women's clothing and makeup in the dream and he was gay; a homosexual. His hair was very low cut and dyed blonde. If you type in Amber Rose in Google, the very first picture of her very low cut blonde hair is exactly how this young man was rocking his hair. He wore red lipstick and pencilled in eyebrows. Oh man I can't remember the colour of the sleeveless top he was wearing but it was a very light colour. Maybe very light yellow to white but don't quote me. He wore black and white floral pants and trust me fam and people; he was hot; truly good looking. If you saw him you would want to date him to how gorgeous he was. Man did he ever have a big booty. His booty was big and fit his body type and shape. Yes the brother was fine; hot. In the dream, I knew his brother and or family member but he did not know I knew his brother and or family member. See in the dream this very gorgeous young black man was swindling money from his brother and or family member. His brother or family member knew someone was taking money from them via his credit card but he did not know who it was. He could not figure out who was stealing from him. I don't know what happened, but in the dream I saw the gorgeous young man using the card; credit card of light green to get money. He took 6 thousand dollars from the credit card and was going to give the money to his boyfriend. All the money that this young man took went to his boyfriend because he the young man wanted to ruin his brother and or family member. I cannot tell you why he wanted to ruin his brother and or family member because in the dream I was not told why nor was I shown why. So now when I saw this; this young man taking the money from his brother's and or family member's credit card, I wanted to tell the brother and or family member what was happening. I befriended the young man and put my arm in his arm and told him he was gorgeous; pretty. I wanted him to feel like I wanted to date him so that I could tell his brother and or family member he was cheating the truth. So we walked a short bit and he caught up with his friends. That's when he showed me his skin by lifting up his sleeveless shirt and said, look at me; I am not pretty. He squat down and in doing so you could see his huge ass that was slightly disproportionate but fit his body anyway. And I woke up out of my sleep. I cannot go back to sleep because this dream kept nagging me. Fam and people, I was up at around 4 am, did the dishes and cleaned the inside of the fridge amongst other things. Ate something because I was so hungry Forced myself back to sleep a couple of hours later to have this dream nagging the hell out of me since after nine am December 21, 2015.

If you Google floral black and white pants you will see what I am talking about and the third picture of Amber Rose is the exact complexion the young man had.

So no, I am so not going to try to decipher this dream. He was dressed as female and it could be a female doing this to a family member or spouse. Thus I've told you in some of these books; dreams do not walk straight. They are crooked and you have to decipher them. I just have to watch and see and I am so not going to. Whoever this dream is for, the person will get it and all will be revealed; fall into place. They will figure it out and take the necessary actions to protect their Visa or Master Card and or bank account; finances so that this person cannot rob them again. Yes I've been seeing more and more theft lately and I truly do not know why.

So I have to ask Lovey, what do you want me to do? Do you want me to bring down sentencing on thieves and if so what is the right and true punishment for them; thieves?

I know what I want and need to do Lovey, but is this truly what you want? I know stealing is a sin and it does hurt; cause pain for all who are involved. But why would this guy in my dream want to destroy his or her family like that?

You are stealing from your family to give to your lover and this is truly wrong; a sin. What did your family member do to deserve this from you?

If it is lawful Lovey and if it is thy will Lovey, this is the punishment I would hand down for thieves on our behalf. No one should steal but it happens I know. We all take what do not belong to us Lovey including you. Meaning we all take from you; steal from you.

No don't with me. Yes I went there because when we cheat on you with other god and gods including idols, we are taking away our good up good up self from you. Thus cheat is stealing and I am sure you know of the song; "STEALING LOVE ON THE SIDE." I need not say *more when it comes to this. When a clergy member; preacher or pastor, pope or bishop, deacon and parishioner preach and teach lies about you Lovey, they are stealing truth away from you. They are robbing you Lovey of your good and true people.*

If a person steal food or money to feed his or her family due to the neglect of his or her own political leaders (Presidents or Prime Ministers) of the land he or she lives in, then the political leaders of the land he or she reside in must be charged for neglect and abandonment; sin. They the political leaders of the land must be charged for theft and not the person stealing. As a government official you caused your citizen to go out there and rob and steal to put food on his or her table to feed their family; thus causing shame to him or her and their family. You took an oath to look after your people and you abandoned your oath and duty to your citizens; people.

However Lovey, if it is not the fault of the government (political leaders) that this person go out and steal, then the government cannot be held responsible or accountable for this person's thievery.

And Lovey, please do not let me contradict myself from another book. Yes I know some governments globally provide funds to help their citizens financially. One such government is Canada and sometimes the little you get cannot stretch the way you want it to, but you know what Lovey, they are trying and you cannot knock a country for trying. Sometimes we as citizens are too greedy. Some don't work but expect to get all. **So truly look at fairness in all that you do because in truth, we cannot blame the government for all that is wrong and unfair in our lives.** We can't expect them (the government) to give us everything. They have bills to pay just like everyone else. And we as the poor cannot expect the government to tax the wealthy more than they are already taxed to feed us.

As citizens we cannot be breeding machines an ha fifty one million pickney fi fifty one million different men.

We have a responsibility to self; thus many of us are to be blamed for the financial difficulties and hardship we get into. If you know you cannot afford to have children truly do not have any.

If you know you and your family are tight; good, truly do not steal from them to give to a shirt or skirt; male or female because at the end of the day when he or she is gone, who do you truly have left come on now?

I know some men and women train and teach their children to go out there and rob people. For you the parent (s) that does this; condemnation and sin is truly on you. You must be severely punished and all must be taken from you. You cannot be given repentance of sin for this sin. You knowingly and willingly teach your child to do wrong. Thus parent (s) and child and or children are guilty of sin and your names must be recorded in the book of thieves. This sin cannot be removed from the sin record of thieves no matter how hard you try. You are not forgiven and never will be forgiven for this willful sin. You know you are wrong and you continue with doing your wrongs anyway. Thus this is a willful sin and willful sins are truly not forgiven.

Identity theft should never be forgiven either Lovey. This act is a condemnation and curse; true sin and curse Lovey. Thus make it so. You do not go out of your way to take another human being identity; right to life on this earth and in the spiritual realm and say it is yours from them. Look at the pain and suffering you are causing that person. They are going through hell whilst you're killing them; robbing them of everything. Who the bleep are you to do this come on now?

Look at the hell that person have to face in order to prove their right here on earth. All that you've done; taken from them they now have prove that your wrongs is not them. You stole their birth certificate to life and hand them death and for this you must be condemned and cursed for life more than forevermore come on now. Your children must now bare your pain and suffering because they are going to suffer because of you. Just as you robbed that person of their well being everything must be taken from your children and you. No repentance of sin is given because you sat there, schemed and or plotted how to rob these people of their birthright; identity. You took their life and left them in hell; ruin. So no, all must be taken from you and your *children forever ever without end more than infinitely and indefinitely. You willingly and knowingly caused another human being severe hurt and pain. Thus you must pay and your children must pay including their children's children. That person did you no harm or wrong but you maliciously and willingly erred them. And don't you dare go there Lovey because humans have and has done the same thing to you. Look how hard you have it with humanity. They the Babylonians stole your identity and look at what it cost our good and true people then and now.*

Look at how low men have cast you.

Babylon stole our identity Lovey. Now tell me, what truth and true lineage does the black race have?

No tell me Lovey, tell me where is our place with you?

Have we not lost it because of the Babylonians of old? Are we still not losing our place with you because OF THE RELIGIONS OF MEN; CLERGY?

You are our right and god Lovey, but yet we are being raped of our rights and identity. Our home have become tainted and polluted because they brought sin and deceit into our land; home. Look at the beauty we had in you and with you. Where is that beauty now Lovey? Go back to Moses and read what happened to our people in man's so called holy book. How many of our people died because of Babylon?

How many of our people are dying and being led to the slaughter house of death by modern day Babylon and Judas's that have not our best interest at heart?

Look at what the clergy have and has done to you.

Look at the so called royals of the globe; how they profess royalty; their royal lineage when 99.99% of them is truly not of you. They cannot trace their lineage back to you but yet they claim royalty; to be royal. Yes there is more, and for you that's going to try with the 99.99% due to numerology; truly don't because your bullshit is truly not needed here.

Onwards I go because I've strayed yet again.

I know Lovey some children jus dyam bad; thus the punishment for these children below.

If a land is governed by Kings and Queens, Emperors, Prince or Princesses and they cause their citizens to go out there and rob and steal to put food on their table; then they must be stripped indefinitely of their title. An anyway Lovey, some a dem a nuh real royalty. Dem jus gi demself di name; steal your children's birthright for real.

They cause their people to go hungry and unfed thus causing them; their people and or citizens to steal. So they must lose it all and their children and children's children must lose it all also for more than infinite and indefinite lifetimes and generations without end to come. No government official, king or queen, prince and princesses must rob their people and others of their fundamental right and rights to life; food, shelter and clothing including water. You say you govern, then govern right and provide true and just for your people; citizens. These people are your people and they are trusting you with their lives; thus do right and good by them by providing for them right and good. No one in your land should go hungry if you have good and true governance.

Lovey, this also goes for the clergy of the globe. As a matter of fact, no clergy represent you. **<u>People just give their lives foolishly to them for a place to belong.</u> Thus I am hoping that you bring every clergy member and church member that believe and practice in the shit and crap; cesspools of sin called religion to their knees. Hell is their home thus many hath no repentance of sin from you Lovey for the lies they've told, preach and teach including believe in when it comes to you.** *Death is their father; thus death will deal with them real soon I know this for sure.*

If a man or woman including child willingly and knowingly go out there and steal for stealing sake they must get caught right away Lovey. They either pay for the things they've taken when caught or a family member pay for the things they've taken. If no payment can be made by that individual or family; then that child or person must work off their debt free of charge. So if the debt is $100.00 then that child or person must work for free 100 hours hard labour. So if the person you stole from say you must clean filth with your toothbrush, you must clean the filth in his home or place of business with your toothbrush without complaint.

Whatever that person requires you to do for that 100 hours you must do and do well.

And no, he or she cannot say use the toothbrush afterwards nor can they ask for sexual favours or anything of the sort as payment. If he or she say you must iron his or her clothes you must do so without complaint. If the child is a minor then mother, father, grandmother, sister, brother, cousin or grandfather must work and pay off the debt for that child. If he or she (your debtor) asks you to brush your teeth with the dirty toothbrush or wash yourself with the same dirty toothbrush you used to clean filth then your contract with them (your debtor) is null and void. And they (your debtor) must be the ones to clean their teeth and or mouth with the filthy toothbrush. And if you lie to get out of your punishment, Lovey must turn your lies back on you right away and your punishment be doubled and you will become the slave of your debtor literally.

Punishment is the sole responsibility of the person you stole from if you or your family cannot pay for what you've taken. And no, your debtor cannot be unreasonable nor can they over charge you for the goods you've taken.

And yes the same law applies if it's money you stole from that person or anyone.

I know some of you are saying this is truly not fair, but it is. What I did not give you is the age limit; thus I am glad I did not upload this book on Lulu.com yet.

The law only applies to minors. If your child and or family member is over the age of consent, mother, father, sister, brother, cousin, grandmother and grandfather is not responsible to bare or bear the burden and hardship for that child. So if the legal age of consent is 16, then parents or guardian; legal guardian cannot be made to pay back or work for that child's debtor. So depending on country, province, state, district, know your age of consent because it is different from country to country and state to state. To further add to this, the 3 strike rule applies. If the child continue to steal, after 3 strikes he or she is out; they have to bare their own burden because the age of consent becomes null and void. They are stealing on purpose come on now. And yes, I know some kids you can talk to them till yu blue inna yu face; dem naah listen. They do their own thing anyway. I know because I have some. Good guardianship some kids do not want therefore I know the difficulty and difficulties some of you as parents are going through. Some a dem pickney ya, as parents yu caane talk to dem. Lord have mercy because I am a true testament of this one. Wow, but you know what, let me continue on because I truly do not have it easy raising my children by myself. Some man anuh man to yass.

Some a unnu tink sey because unnu a pay child support that's it for you as a father or mother because some women do pay child support for their children. That's not it. Be there emotionally for your child and or children as well. Like I said, if you are in prison, use your monthly or weekly phone calls to reach out to your children. Encourage them to stay out of trouble and go to school. Help them with their homework if you can. YOU NEED A SAVING GRACE IN LIFE AND SO DO THEY COME ON NOW. IT'S NOT ALL ABOUT YOU, IT'S ABOUT THEM ALSO. No child asked to come into this world. We are the ones to bleep and get them, so dyam well tek care a dem. Some a unnu burden unnu parents and grandparents dem wit unnu responsibility and this has to stop come on now. And don't you dare go there with what I said above.

Recently my son and I (the second one) were talking about parenting in this family and man did he ever tell me some things. Yes negative. He also told me the same thing about children. He said, no child asked to come into this world and he is right. So it's our responsibility as parents to take care of them; our children. Yes, some of us burden our children and at times I do due to illness. Hence sickness is a bitch sometimes; well all the time. Loathe and despise sickness with every fabric of my being. No fam and people come on now. Sickness take away from your life and brings closer to death. So yes, I loathe and despise sickness. As a parent I do my best with them (my children) and sometimes you feel like your best isn't good enough, but it is good enough.

As parents we cannot choose our children's friends; they have to choose their friends for themself. Thus negative influences do come into their lives and negative influences do influence them. Yes I am grateful and blessed because as a single parent Lovey has always been there for me including my mother. So in many ways, I am so not a single parent because I had good family members in the living and in the spiritual realm looking out for me and helping me.

Strayed again

Don't teach your child bad come on now. Some children are your saving grace, so help them to save you with the good you do for them. I complain about my kids because dem mek it hard pan mi, but I am not giving up on them. I bug Lovey for them. Yes I want to move away from them because they don't want life the easy way. Some of them not all. If I am telling you and showing you how hot the fire is, why the hell would you let someone come and tell you otherwise? Why listen to them call me a liar? I do not lie to you, so why be like Eve; Evening? Didn't Lovey tell Eve about him and she did not listen to Lovey as recorded in man's book of sin and ungodliness?

She disobeyed and look what happened.

She got kicked out of Lovey's abode.
She felt pain in everything that she did.

She had to work her ass off now didn't she?

She suffered hard before she died and she did die.

She's the one to receive her disobedient children in hell.

She's the one sitting at the gate of hell receiving you and you have to tell her you love her upon entry. This is how I saw it and this is how I am relating it back to you.

So, if you know disobedience gets you ejected from the realm of Lovey indefinitely, why do all to get to hell?

Change your dirty ways and or your dirty linen of self. I've told you, spiritual fire is hotter than the fire or heat of the sun. So why strive to get to hell?

We know there is fire in both realms. Earthly fire takes away from the life of earth; all and spiritual fire kills you; is your final death. So protect your life all around and or in both realms come on now.

I cannot save those that Lovey has not given me. So if you are not his child; then I cannot save you if I am the saving grace for humanity.

*Like I've said and will forever say, **LOVEY DID NOT GIVE ANYONE OF US DEATH, WE ARE THE ONES TO GIVE UP OUR LIVES FOOLISHY TO DEATH.** We listen to others tell us crap about Lovey and life. People that has not your best interest at heart.*

If you truly love a person, why the hell would you want to give them death?

Why give them up if you don't have to?

Come on now tell me.

I truly love you, why take you the one that I truly love out of my life to live a life of suffaration an haadship?

Dat mek sense?

Lovey a gi mi life easy, mi fi lef easy life fi haadship!!

Mi naah fi wuk because Lovey has and have given me all the help that I need. Mi naahfi lif straw. All I have to do is ensure that I am clean. All is taking care of around me; so why would I give up the good up good up goodness of life and prosperity Lovey a gimmi fi goh jain death? Auta mi nuh mad. I have to dirty myself and life unclean; live by the filth of the demons of hell when I accept death. So why would I want to go there? I have no say or choice in anything in hell. All is dictated to you and you are controlled. In hell you cannot step out of line. You have to do as the demons of hell say day in and day out.

With Lovey I'm always clean and smelling right. In hell you have to sit with your enemies, talk to dem, even lay with dem. Yuk. And if you complain about anything, you are severely punished and laughed at. Hell no. So why the hell should I strive to go to hell knowing all this?

all the lies you tell, all the lives you're taken in the name of death; war with your man made diseases and war machines, you must pay for. THUS MODERN DAY SODOM AND GOMORRAH (Jamaica and the United States of America) must be destroyed. Thus saith the Lord thy God meaning it is so. Your spiritual bank account (upward eye in the triangle) must be turned down to you and brought to naught. Allelujah

Just as your physical bank account is naught; in the negative trillions, so must your spiritual bank account be and it is.

The upward eye in triangle must be taken from you because you've done more than wickedness in the sight of God and Man. You're a walking disgrace to Life, thus Satan and or Death loves you so.

*<u>**You give Satan power; thus you kill for death and leave your land and people bankrupt without knowing that all you did for death, he was bankrupting you and bringing your land and people to your knees.**</u> You are so indebted to death that nothing; absolutely nothing can or will save you. Thus saith the Lord thy God meaning it is so.*

You are officially stripped of your title. You no longer have life; spiritual life (the upward eye in triangle). You kill life not just at home but globally. So because of this, life must be taken from your land and people and you must pay for the evils you have done from past to present including pay for the evils of your tomorrow.

Life must go back home because land and people hath none. You are the living, breathing and walking dead.

You've given death your life thus death must take land and people on a massive scale. All that you've done, you've forgotten that ***EVERY LAND OF LOVEY EVIL WAS GOING TO DESTROY. YOU AMERICA, THE UNITED STATES OF AMERICA GOT SPIRITUAL LIFE, TRUE LIFE IN THE SPIRITUAL REALM HERE ON EARTH AND YOU DID NOT KEEP THIS LIFE SAFE. YOU ACCEPTED DEATH, THUS DEATH DESTROYED YOU AND YOUR LIFE LITERALLY JUST AS IT DID DESTROY JUDAH AND THE LIFE OF JUDAHITES GLOBALLY. BUT NOT ALL JUDAHITES WERE DESTROYED.*** *Some of Judah was saved but Israel was not saved; all bowed down to death; worshipped and praised death and now death is going to take you home on a massive scale.*

And I am so going to interrupt this book again.

Yesterday, (it's not yesterday anymore because I am editing this book) *I dreamt my family and daughter's friends. Her friend had this weird black and white tiger. It wasn't really a tiger, it was a crossbreed animal that more resembled a horse or donkey mixed with a dog. Weird I know. Apparently my son (second child) made a mess and I was cleaning up his mess (feces and or shit) off the floor and some got on my hand. I went into the kitchen and* showed my daughter and told her to wipe it off. Beside the stove in the kitchen someone was frying egg on the floor. I had another family member from my grandmother's side in the kitchen with me and he was cooking also. My daughter was still in the kitchen with me and it was then that I noticed the brown tray with eggs she had in her hand. People I don't know but she cracked some of the eggs about four I believe and she was frying them on the dirty kitchen floor. And no for those of you who are wondering, there was no heat or fire. I know what this dream means. I cleaned off the balcony. It had dog poop on it and I did get some on my hands. The eggs my daughter was cooking ended up being her washroom flooding. She didn't know it was flooded. It was when the super came to tell us the downstairs people are complaining about water coming into their apartment we knew. Funny, the day before she came home and saw the washroom flooded and I thought it was her brother that flooded it. She fixed the problem but it was not her brother; thus I have to let him know and apologize to him for thinking it was him that bonged up the toilet.

This morning my dream world had to do with good values. Kept dreaming about goodness virtually all night and I had to tell Lovey about goodness.

Goodness must prevail and all must be good and true in our world. I am truly not concerned about evil anymore because I am trusting Lovey to keep all facets of wickedness and evil away from us; his good and true own. Goodness cannot be weak people; thus good must separate from all who are wicked and evil. Everything must be good and true down to the seeds he Lovey has and have given me.

He knows I cannot plant these seeds in a dirty planet filled with wicked and evil people. Yes the message can be given right away right now but it's truly up to him. I've told him, we must know the full truth of everything. He must let humanity know the full truth right away and he's not listening to me. Humanity must know the truth despite some of them not being able to be saved. Some did willingly give their lives over to death and some let others talk them into baptizing in blood; death.

But but but some of you are saying. Lovey gave us all life and no one can baptize in life. Life is given and we are to live it good and true; clean.

We knew the devil was going to lead us astray, but we forgot. We were so caught up in the lies and sins of evil that we forgot about life; our own life and the life of others. And don't go there about your country. **_"THOU SHALT NOT KILL."_**

If we truly loved Lovey and abided by his law and laws of truth and cleanliness death would not reach us.

KNOW THIS; **_DEATH CANNOT COME INTO YOUR LIFE WITHOUT BEING INVITED._**

DEATH IS LIKE A VAMPIRE. IF YOU DON'T LET A VAMPIRE IN YOUR HOME CAN HE OR SHE COME IN?

NO RIGHT?

So why are you letting death into your life and or home to kill you?

LOVEY DEALS NOT IN BLOOD.

LOVEY DEAL IN WATER.

WATER IS THE PUREST FORM OF LIFE BECAUSE WATER NURISHES; SAVES IN REALMS, THE PHYSICAL AND SPIRITUAL.

DEATH DEAL (S) IN BLOOD; THUS BLOOD CAN KILL YOU AND IT DOES KILL BILLIONS. YOUR BLOOD CAN BE TAINTED, BUT THE TRUE WATERS OF LIFE CANNOT BE TAINTED.

WATER IS LIFE; SPIRITUAL AND PHYSICAL LIFE. BLOOD IS DEATH AND THIS IS WHY THE CLERGY GLOBALLY TELLS YOU TO ACCEPT BLOOD BY BAPTIZING YOU IN BLOOD. THEY ALSO TELL YOU TO DRINK BLOOD SO THAT YOU CAN TAINT YOUR SPIRIT.

WHEN YOU BABTIZE IN BLOOD YOU ARE ACCEPTING DEATH. SO WHEN YOU DIE (THE SHEDDING OF FLESH FROM SPIRIT) AND IT MATTERS NOT IF YOU ARE GOOD OR BAD YOU MUST GO TO HELL; DIE.

YOU ACCEPTED DEATH IN THE LIVING AND BECAUSE OF THIS ACCEPTANCE YOUR NAME IS WRITTEN IN DEATH'S BOOK OF DEATH.

Listen, my children were baptized and christened and I did seek repentance for this and tore up their baptismal certificate.

I DID NOT KNOW THE TRUTH AND WHEN I FOUND OUT THE TRUTH, I WENT TO LOVEY WITH REPENTENCE. I ASKED LOVEY TO FORGIVE ME OF THIS AND I KNOW HE'S FORGIVEN ME BECAUSE I AM STILL WRITING FOR HIM. Lovey didn't choose death for us, we chose death for self. You're getting the truth as given to me and as I know it; look into things and save yourself. Save your children so that they can intern save you for hell and death.

I know the truth and true love of my Beloved; Mother, and I have to do all that I can in goodness and in truth to save her.

I also know the truth and true love of my Beloved; Lovey, and I have to do all that I can in goodness and in truth to save him.

I truly do not want or need my children or anyone for that matter to be tied; well married to death in this way or in any way for that matter.

Listen people, I truly need my loved ones to be saved.

I need the seeds that Lovey has and have given me to be planted true and clean. No wormy wormy (worms) must these fruits have in them. These seeds must grow up good, clean and honest and truly organic. The fruits and or food that come from them must be good, clean, honest and true for the body and environment. Not one bad fruit ever must come from these trees.

These seeds that I plant for Lovey and with Lovey are good, true, pure and honest, truly peaceful and harmonious, truly loving and void of all sin and sins including evil will. So therefore, the fruits must be truly loving, good, harmonious, truly peaceful, pure, and void of all sin and sins including evil will. Everyone must work in unison with the environment; land and or Mother Earth, you Lovey, Nature including the good universe and spiritual realm. If something is going to harm the environment, then that something or someone should not be produced or be born. Goodness cannot beget evil; goodness must infinitely and indefinitely forever ever without end produce all that is clean, honest, good and true, pure, healthy and wise forever ever without end from generation unto generation continually without end. We cannot go hungry or broke because we will produce enough and sometimes a little more to feed us and only us. Wicked and evil people we will not provide for because the wicked and evil take from life and destroy all that is good and true including you Lovey. So no, good is forbidden more than indefinitely to feed the wicked and evil no matter how poor or destitute they look; seem.

When good give their prosperity to evil, good loses their prosperity because all evil does; evil try to eliminate that good person.

So no, let the wicked and evil fend for themself Lovey.

And in all that you do Lovey, truly protect our good and true own so that no evil can or will reach them come on now.

No sickness of diseases must come from us either Lovey. So in all that you do Lovey, eliminate sickness more than infinitely and indefinitely and more than forever ever without end from your mountain and my mountain of good and true life. This mountain is now our good and true mountain and absolutely no sickness must be on this mountain or come from this mountain ever again come on now. You see the way I struggle with ill health, so no, sickness must be eliminated forever ever without end from us and our domain. I truly do not need sickness because sickness takes away from our good up good up life and bring us in the hands of death.

Sickness take away our energy and slowly kill us. So no, no more sickness ever again my Beloved. I truly cannot take sickness anymore.

Wicked and evil people cannot enjoy our goodness because nothing is produced for them. Our god (you Lovey) is not the god of wicked and evil people; so we know not the wicked and evil of the globe anymore come on now.

So this morning December 23, 2015 my dream world has been different. I truly do not know what I am forgetting and or what I am missing. Dreamt Shaquille O'Neal. He was with me and he made me late for my graduation. Shaq was dressed in white people; thus the devil is coming at me again. If you've read in one of my earlier books about the black king dressed in white in the month of December; then you know that male devils come in white clothing in the month of December for me and I truly don't know why. This is also a dream in a dream; **thus some blacks are white and some whites are black. This is confusing for you; thus the dream world is truly confusing and distorted in many ways.**

Shaq represents a white male in the living for me. And yes seeing females you know in the past can represent a male. So you truly have to know the spiritual realm.

And infinitely yes; this is how things get twisted and misinterpreted in the physical realm.

December is the 13th month yes, but why is it so deadly for me? Why is there so much death in December Lovey?

THUS WE TRULY NEED TO MAKE DECEMBER TRULY CLEAN AND PURE AND VOID OF ALL DEATH AND SINS.

No Lovey, this is truly our month, so why is death destroying it for us?

Why do Death have to take so many lives in December?

Decemba annu death's month, so let's evict death from taking lives in this month period. All other months' death can have but truly not December come on now Lovey.

Lovey are we not the first and the last?

No for real Lovey. Humans cannot comprehend the first and the last; thus they associate the first and the last to Jesus the son of death.

THE FIRST AND THE LAST HAS NOTHING TO DO WITH JESUS. IT HAS ALL TO DO WITH CAPRICORNS. WE ARE THE FIRST AND THE LAST. WE ARE THE FIRST MONTH OF THE YEAR AND THE LAST MONTH OF YEAR WITH THE FIRST MONTH BEING JANUARY AND THE LAST MONTH BEING DECEMBER. NOW YOU KNOW THE TRUTH OF THE FIRST AND THE LAST AS TALKED ABOUT IN YOUR SO CALLED HOLY BOOK; BIBLE.

So yes, Shaq in the dream made me late for my graduation; high school graduation from the looks of it.

When I arrived, Debbie (black Debbie and not white Debbie) was excited to see me. She hugged me and said, "Michelle's here everyone."

See they were giving out diplomas by last name and those that were graduating were standing in line to go up the small set of stairs to get their diploma, but I missed getting my diploma. I wasn't there to hear my name call; so I missed graduation all together in that sense.

So when Debbie said, "Michelle's here everyone," this dutty stinking dibi dibi wrenking gyal (I believe she was Babylonian) but black said something rude embarrassing me. She was on the podium I believe but don't quote me. But people heard what she said. Her words hurt me so much that I gathered my things and left; said I am leaving to Debbie. I told her I am embarrassed; she embarrassed me. So I left and Shaq who was dressed in white came after me and tried making the funnies so that I would cheer up. It's weird, but he had on these roller skates that had I think a fluffy ball or stuffed animal on it. The roller skates was fast and it did look funny. He caught up to me and told me he loved me and I thought it odd because he was with someone else. It's like it's implied that he always loved me. Then I woke up out of my sleep. People now you know me and love; **"thus Shaq fuck you royally with your fake ass love."** Kiss my natural brown ass with your love bullshit. Yes I know this creep is the devil; death in disguise and it truly won't work. Shaq yo mama need I say more.

So truly fuck you death and the devil for using Shaq in your nasty game of ketch har fi kill har bullshit. I know that wasn't Shaq, so truly sod off and leave me the fuck alone. You White and Black Death go chuck literally because I condemn and seal your corrupt asses in hell more than infinitely and indefinitely and more than forever ever without end for the bullshit that you just pulled. Stay with your demons because you're truly not wanted or needed. Get a fucking clue because you're both rejected. No means fucking no in my book come on now.

I truly don't want your love so truly don't go there. Love is death and from you telling me you Love me you can chuck. Mi anuh Eve; Evening suh clear off bitch, you can't play me. Remember Eve; Evening pickney haffi tell har sey dem love har at the gates of hell.

Mi nuh want yu love, kip eeee because mi an yu anuh fren. I TRULY DO NOT BELONG TO YOU NOR WILL I ABANDON LOVEY FOR YOU. SO TRULY AND DULY KISS MY NATURAL BROWN ASS FOR REAL.

FUCK OFF
FUCK OFF
FUCK OFF
AND FUCK YOU TOO

Gi yu pickney dem yu fake ass love and truly don't come around me with it. Lovey is my true love; thus Lovey has my truth and true love including true unison and devotion. A im mi si an a im mi cuss wen things aren't going my way. Now tell mi, a mi fi gi up fimi bunnunoonus more than sweet fry dumpling and ackee and salt fish not to mention millie mango and jackfruit, my clean and clear drinking water of good up good up good and true life fi yu? Buoy goh sidung yu hear. Who the fuck are you?

Don't get me crass dis mauning because mi wi cuss out wey nuh lef inna yu dis mauning. Don't try with me and Lovey because you're a fucking disgrace to life and death. You fucking stink and rude bout...watchya man I DON'T NEED YOUR FUCKING REUNION. I AM UNITED WITH LOVEY ALREADY; SO KEEP YOUR SHIT AND BULLSHIT OF REUNION, I TRULY DON'T NEED IT.

Yes nice try, but it will not work. KNOW THIS BITCH AND ASSHOLE, LOVEY DON'T DEAL IN REUNIONS; WE ARE ALREADY UNITED, REUNIONS WE TRULY DO NOT DO BECAUSE WE ARE ALREADY TOGETHER.

Thus Reunion Africa is truly off my to go to vacation list with you Lovey. Dis man dyam bright eeee Lovey.

We are bonded and im want mi fi break my bond with you. SO TRULY THANK YOU LOVEY FOR TRULY LETTING ME MISS MY GRADUATION AND REUNION

WITH DEATH. THUS NO REUNITING ME WITH DEATH; BOTH MALE AND FEMALE.

AND LOVEY, IN ALL THAT WE DO FOR EACH OTHER; NO REUNION OF ANY SORT OR KIND WITH DEATH MORE THAN INFINITELY AND INDEFINITELY MORE THAN FOREVER EVER WITHOUT END.

GOOD CANNOT REUNITE WITH DEATH UNDER ANY CIRCUMSTANCES AND DEATH CANNOT REUNITE WITH GOOD UNDER ANY CIRCUMSTANCES MORE THAN INFINITELY AND INDEFINITELY FOREVER EVER WITHOUT END.

SO ALL DEFENCES MUST GO UP SO THAT WE CAN NEVER EVER WITHOUT END REUNITE WITH DEATH AND HIS AND HER WICKED AND EVIL PEOPLE. THE FRAMEWORKS AND DEFENCES MUST BE MORE IMPENETRABLE THAN THAT OF THE SPIRITUAL REALM; THAT WHICH SEPARATE GOOD FROM EVIL.

Evil is more than indefinitely cut off from us. And Lovey, no one can come and break these defences down; not even my children. Lock out is indefinite and more than forever ever without end. NO REUNION WITH DEATH

AND EVIL; ALL THAT IS WICKED AND EVIL PERIOD. NOT EVEN YOU LOVEY CAN OVERRIDE MY GOOD AND TRUE WILL IN THIS MATTER.

I am overriding you. Yes I know you are God; my gorgeous and beautiful Lovey and beloved, but this one I have true say on and not you. It's my good and true will my darling and beloved and truly true Lovey; Good God and Allelujah.

Don't because you are my true beloved period hence you are my Lovey.

Onwards I go because I've strayed big time.

Keeping with the law for badass kids that is written above; INFINITELY AND INDEFINITELY NO, THIS LAW DOES NOT APPLY TO SCAMMERS AND BANK ROBBERS; THIS LAW IS FOR BAD ASS KIDS ONLY. There are no contradictions here, so death truly don't try with me. No is no. You are rejected, so truly stay the hell away from me because I did condemn you and seal your condemned ass in hell.

For banks, major corporations and bank robbers and yes scammers that scam people out of their hard earned money, then your punishment must be truly severe and from generation unto generation without end. You must be condemned and cursed more than infinitely and indefinitely forever ever without end. You cannot rob a man or woman including child; anyone of what rightfully belong to them. So yes your children must lose it all and their children's children must lose it all. None can recover from this condemnation and sin; thus your debt and their debt none of you can repay. And when a good person can say, I will repay the debt of this child for their family providing that this child repentant and give his or her word of truth that he or she will not steal and or take what does not belong to him or her ever again; this good will and gesture is not given to banks or corporation, bank robbers and scammers that willingly and knowingly steal. All of you know better thus practice good accounting and have good accountability. Numbers do not lie, therefore none of you should falsify your books or steal from anyone. Life and death records lie not on anyone; nor does it steal from you or anyone come on now. **No one should steal to steal.** *Ask, and if it can be given you will get come on now. Like I've told you Lovey, what I put away financially for you and our people including land and lands; no one must come and take a cent; penny.*

Not one penny must be stolen from our bank account, and if one penny is stolen; rain down hail as big as footballs and basketballs on the land and people of the person who stole from us. Let the land become so dark and barren that not even di sun shine. I am not joking around nor am I dicking around with anyone when it comes to what I've given you and put away for our future and the future of our land (s) and people; generations. We've been through too much fi people and or someone to steal from us. So guard us and our property and wealth including good up good up health with more than your life Lovey. Ours, hell no with wicked and evil people; they were not there for us. All they did was keep me down so that I could not give you your true needs and wants. So no, I am truly not having it. Why the hell should someone and or anyone come along and cause another human being or company pain like this?

It's bad enough that we spy on people; each other and turn peeping toms. What the hell do I need to know what you are doing for?

Bleep you, you want to build arms and nuclear weapons go right ahead and do it, but Lovey had better cause the earth and all the elements of the earth and universe to detonate those bombs and nuclear weapons on your condemned asses. Why the bleep live to kill come on now?

Why the hell should Earth and the Universe live with your condemned asses?

You're not just hurting human life; you're hurting earthly and spiritual life you morons and jezebels.

Fuck you; kill your damn self. Why the fuck should someone die for your hateful and condemned asses?

You value not life; so why the fuck should life and or Lovey value you?

You design and create to take life; so why the hell should life have anything to do with you?

You take away human life, earthly life, spiritual life, the life of God; Lovey, den have di gaul to want a saving grace in life. YOU KILL LIFE, SO WHY SHOULD LIFE SAVE YOU?

KNOW THIS; LIFE WILL NEVER EVER SAVE YOU BECAUSE YOU TAKE FROM LIFE LITERALLY.

ALL YOU AND YOUR PEOPLE ARE GOING TO FIND IS DEATH AND DEATH COMES SHORTLY ON A MASSIVE SCALE COME ON NOW.

WE ALL HAD A CHOICE.

LOVEY GAVE US THE RIGHT TO CHOOSE LIFE OR DEATH DUE TO WILL AND BILLIONS OF YOU CHOSE DEATH OVER LIFE. SO DIE BECAUSE DEATH WAS YOUR CHOICE. Don't cry now that death is taking you.

You lived for death and you let false people; liars that call themselves prophets; woops profits, messengers of God; woops messengers of death, politicians, kings and queens, the clergy and Babylonians rob you of your right to life.

Dem tell wi sey to honour our father an madda that thy days be long according to what is written in man's nasty and onholy book, an wi nuh listen. Pickney a fight gainst madda an faada. Lovey but more importantly, look at what we did to you and all you've given us here on earth and in the universe. We truly do not honour you. Instead with fight against you and destroy and kill all you've given us to live by.

We pollute self and waterways including this earth and universe.

We go against you and look at us now.

Tell me something Lovey, if you did not love us true; would you give us an abundance of food and water here on earth for us to live and find our way back to you?

We as humans divorced you for good here on earth and instead of saying let me clean myself up and show Lovey we appreciate what he's done for us; we side with death against him and take all from him including our good up good up life.

Everything yu tell wi nuffi du, wi du.

Now let me ask you something, GOODNESS FI BOUNCE HAFFA PEOPLE AN EVIL AND OR BAD STICK?

No Lovey for real, goodness fi bounce haffa people an only evil and or badness stick?

No

Well eee seem suh inna my book. Evil had their time and the time of evil is up. It's time to repel evil and send evil back to where it came from come on now.

It's time for good and true people to live now Lovey man come on now. So truly start the process of our true and good living come on now.

ALL EVIL MUST BOUNCE OFF GOOD AND TRUE PEOPLE; THE GOOD AND TRUE THAT ARE TRULY TRYING TO BECOME CLEAN SO THAT WE CAN GET TO YOU AND OR REACH YOU IN TRUTH AND TRUE PEACE. GOODNESS BEGETS GOODNESS LOVEY, SO LET THE GOOD AND TRUE TRULY LIVE GOOD AND TRUE COME ON NOW.

Life; good and true life is indefinite Lovey; without end. So let true and good life reign now. You can no longer allow evil to destroy and kill us come on now.

This earth and universe can no longer accommodate evil and wicked people come on now. The wages of sin is death, so why are you prolonging the life of death here on earth and in the universe Lovey?

Yes, I know we were the ones that did not listen and we are still not listening. As nations of people and black people we truly do not listen to good counsel and this non and or not listening behaviour have to stop. The penalty of death is truly not worth it come on now.

YOU CANNOT CONTINUE TO LET WICKED AND EVIL SPIRITS AND PEOPLE BLOCK OUR WAY TO YOU LOVEY COME ON NOW.

YOU CANNOT CONTINUE TO LET THEM (WICKED AND EVIL PEOPLE AND SPIRITS) CONTINUE TO USE EVIL AND OR SCIENCE AND OR VOODOO, OBEAH AND WITCHCRAFT AMONGST OTHER EVIL THINGS TO ROB US OF OUR FINANCIAL WELL BEING AND GOOD UP GOOD UP LIFE INCLUDING YOU.

<u>If evil keep robbing us of you Lovey, how can we find you and or get to you?</u>

So yes even though I pray good for my children Lovey, I still want and need to leave them. They need to find life on their own because dem; not all, nah listen to mi.

Mi a get more attitude from mi second son now. Dyam wrenking buoy come tell me sey mi fucking annoying.

Yes people im use di F word to mi, im owna madda. I know I can be annoying, but if I am doing good for you, why get on like that? Yes mi put im inna im place and im bout he was sleeping. I cannot talk to him in his sleep. When you talk to im inna im sleep im wi agree to anything. Yes this has and have happened to many people not just in their sleeping state, but in their drug and alcohol induced state. Yes even in our sick and dying state too. So yes life's a bitch when you are surrounded by wicked and evil people. *Thus evil cannot be good, it can only be true and pure evil; greedy.*

No he was not telling me I am evil by no means, but still im dyam wrenk. So yes if Lovey allows me to, I am going to move thousands of miles from dem an mi si wey dem a goh du.

Yes they are saying I can't live without them because I am sickly, but you know what Lovey; I am trusting you to make a good and clean, including clear way for me so that I will overcome my sickness and ailments. And even if I don't overcome Lovey; please send the good and true; clean help that I need to help me.

Daughter dropped out of College. She said I forced her to go. So yes, I am going to leave her alone Lovey. First child has his college certificates and diploma. He finished his college course this week so he has another college certificate coming and or to get. Yeah him. He knows what he wants and he has achieved the goals he's set for himself. Truly proud of him. Yes I am proud of all my children despite the rude behaviour from some. Just waiting on my last one to graduate high school and better himself.

But with all that said Lovey, I need to move out and away from my children. I need solitude and quiet. I can't take the noise at nights nor can I take the dogs either.

MY GOOD AND TRUE WILL AND I NEED

Oh man the puppy. I have to be the one to wake up and let her out to pee and pooh at nights. I have to feed them and clean off the balcony. Things they are supposed to do they rarely do and I am the one left to do it all.

Lovey, dog nuffi inna house. My children want dogs but yet none can walk them properly or take care of them. I am truly tired and yes I am venting this morning due to my son's friends throwing off my spirit.

My spirit faced it brutal yesterday. Lovey, mi nuh like crosses and mi spirit crass yesterday to the point of near insanity and I cannot deal with this anymore. I cannot condone this bullshit anymore. So yes, I have to move away from my children and let them truly be on their own. I refuse to put my spirit through that again. No parent should have to go through that because of dem pickney fren dem. Some people's spirit are brutal and some people you pick up on them; their false nature.

I was having such a good day yesterday to have it turn into hell by the end of evening and beginning this morning. No come on now. Don't show up unannounced to my home an afta 12 midnight unnu still dey a mi yaade. Mi nuh like unnu, so nuh cum wey mi dey. Unnu nuh hear di old adage, where no bones are provided no dogs are invited. Mi nuh like unnu tan a unnu yaade. Mi fed up a seeing unnu day in and day out and or so often. So yes I truly have to change my life and situation come 2016 for the better.

Yes it's December 19, 2015 and I so can't remember if Jamaica is going to be completely destroyed due to implied vision. Something is going to happen to that land and he did tell me Jamaica is going to be destroyed. So I am waiting to see if that Revelation comes through. Yes it's been a long time coming; so let's see if destruction comes or if a new and better; good change come for Jamaica.

Can't remember if I was at a funeral in my dream state thus the masking of things is truly on again. So I am going to watch for death in my family and not marriage.

I uploaded CONFUSION OR CONFESSION yesterday December 18, 2015 and something is missing from that book in regards to marriage; family and or Royals. Thus this morning I dreamt about Royals. So Lovey, what am I missing in regards to our Royal Lifeline and not bloodline? *__The seeds you've given me to plant over 100 million acres I've made them people. I have to plant the seeds of goodness in the hearts of those you've given me; those that have their name in your book of life.__*

These people are a part of your good and true foundation. They are not from our lineage, lifeline and DNA due to earthly and spiritual descent. But they are your chosen due to cleanliness and truth, thus your true family; children can marry these people. These are the people you've given me but they; these seeds do not share our Royal Lineage and or Lifeline. Man am I making a mockery of this explanation. I truly do not know how to explain it pure and true for the readers of this book to fully comprehend and or over stand. I need the explanation to be clear Lovey so as not to have any confusion in reading and in words.

Royals cannot marry Royals within their family because they share the same DNA and lineage. Thus sister cannot marry sister and brother cannot marry brother.

Father cannot marry daughter and daughter cannot marry father, nor can mother marry daughter and daughter cannot marry mother.

Mother cannot marry son and son cannot marry mother.

Cousins cannot marry cousins because they share the same lifeline; DNA.

Family cannot marry family nor can family lay with family period. It is a sin and it is forbidden.

All in all Lovey and in human terms; **_BLOOD CANNOT MARRY BLOOD PERIOD AND LIFELINE CANNOT MARRY LIFELINE PERIOD._**

I truly hope this makes sense. Explanation complicated but you know what I mean Lovey and I truly hope humans over stand what I am saying to them. *As it is forbidden for family members here on earth to marry family members, it is forbidden for family members that share the same spiritual DNA and genes to marry family members.*

So because I am of your Royal lifeline Lovey, I cannot marry family members of our lifeline and DNA.

Absolutely no one can claim royalty Lovey if they are not of your lifeline and DNA period. Thus many royals that say they are royals are commoners; frauds.

However the seeds you've given me and due to goodness and truth; cleanliness, I can marry because **they do not share our spiritual DNA, Lifeline, Language, Name, Heritage, Lineage, Vibration, Song and Dance; Music and Zone; Home.**

So Lovey, truly let there be no confusion as to what I write when it comes to marriage and Royals.

IF YOU ARE NOT OF LOVEY'S LINEAGE AND LIFELINE; DNA, YOU CANNOT CALL YOURSELF A ROYAL. IT IS FORBIDDEN TO DO SO. SO ALL THOSE PEOPLE GLOBALLY WHO SAY THEY ARE ROYALS; FROM ROYALTY, YOU ARE NOT TRUE ROYALS. YOU ARE MEMBERS OF SOCIETY LIKE EVERYONE ELSE. You are all frauds because you truly do not have Lovey's last name, nor do you share his lifeline and DNA.

If you are not a Lion, Lyon, Lyons you cannot say you have Royal DNA.

None, absolutely none of you can use the Lions, Lyon, Lyons crescent either. The Lions, Lyon, Lyons crescent belongs to us. We are the ones the Lions, Lyon, Lyons flag and crescent represent. It was given to us by our father and none of you should use it. You do not represent the Lions, Lyon, Lyons nor the Lions, Lyon, Lyons represent you. You are not our people and or subjects, so truly use nothing of ours.

Therefore Lovey, every false prophet, false Jew, false royal globally in the different lands that use our flag and condemn us; strip them of their rank and reclaim our flag, take our flag and crescent from them. Truly let it be a condemnation of sin as well as a curse for them to use our flag and crescent and say they are royals when they are truly not.

This crescent belong to us Lovey; so no one outside of true DNA and lifeline (a true Lion, Lyon, Lyons) can use this crescent and flag. And Lovey no wicked and evil Lion, Lyon, Lyons can raise or use our flag and crescent either. And Lovey it matters not if they do not have our last name; they cannot raise this flag and crescent. This flag and crescent must remain pure and clean; thus reclaim our flag and crescent Lovey from the wicked and evil demons of this earth and let's clean them; (flag and crescent) so that they can be made whole; pure and clean once again. No one that is unclean and not of our good and true people; own can put a lion at their gate either for protection and representation. And Lovey let it be truly forbidden for anyone to put their picture beside a lion except for the true Lion, Lyon, Lyons. There are no exceptions Lovey because I know the pride and joy in our good up good up name.

Further, hold this law true for any land that use the eye in the upright triangle to represent their evil and wicked agenda. Humans know not about life; spiritual life, thus no unclean and demonic land is permitted to house the spiritual flag of the eye in the upright triangle.

Life; true life is clean Lovey, humans are not.

Therefore, no unclean land and people must use or can use the flags of life to represent them ever. Evil is not clean, so evil cannot under any circumstances raise our flags of life Lovey and say they represent life; these flags. Evil mock life, kill and destroy life; so absolutely nothing of ours Lovey should be in wicked and evil lands. Everything that we own Lovey belong to our good and true people including the good and true seeds you've given me. So all that we own must stay with our good and true own. This is the law Lovey.

We can no longer share with wicked and evil people including wicked and evil lands; beasts and spirits come on now Lovey.

MY GOOD AND TRUE WILL AND I NEED

Lovey we cannot afford to give away our blessings anymore come on now. Good and evil are more than infinitely and indefinitely separated in the spiritual realm, so let it be this way in the physical realm; here on earth and in the universe as well come on now.

Further, you can no longer provide for the wicked and evil of this earth because the wicked and evil of this earth and universe know not you. They know evil thus they do all that is wicked and evil.

The same goes for the Jamaican flag of Life too Lovey. Absolutely no one that is unclean; this includes unclean demons, spirits and beast; animals can raise this flag and call it their own ever again. This flag represent true life here on earth and it's not to be raised by unclean hands. This flag must stay clean at all times as well.

If you are not clean you cannot wave any of these flags. Condemnation will come upon you and take you without you even knowing it. So I truly suggest the lands and hands that hold and raise these flags; wave them clean self and land up in order to be saved and not be condemned.

Well Jamaica and America is already condemned thus the Flag of Life was taken from Jamaica literally.

Now mi a guh get down pan yu now Lovey because I truly have to.

Lovey, see how far we've come; our trials and tribulations, our hurt and pain, joy and laughter, me nagging you endlessly sometimes, yes even threatening you and forbidding you amongst other things.

Lovey, mi mek yu mi all including punching bag an yu a goh let a shirt tek wey mi accomplish with yu again?

Lovey, yu gi mi di sword of death fi kill death an a black man come eene at di last minute and tek di sword from mi. Now, di young white lady come eene from outside and shi a walk in shit; feces. Shi walk inna di business place wey mi dey an all yu see is a trail of shit; feces behind her. Now mi get di remedy fi clean di shit; feces and mi wash di place clean with this remedy; an di black man tek mi idea anna promote it!!!

Lovey, well mi an yu now because you truly do not get it do you!!!!!

What I give to humanity in these books is of true and good will, but when yu ha crebbay crebbay dutty stinking shirt; black man tekking our glory den wi ha a problem. Who the bleep is this creep?

Who di bleep is him Lovey?

What is mine is ours; yours and mine Lovey. A yu mi cuss time and time again and now yu a goh let this damnation of stench tek di credit fi wey mi du fi yu? No this is truly unreal to regile.

MY GOOD AND TRUE WILL AND I NEED

Lovey, mi look like blurnaught poopunenay to yu?

Wa yu tink mi a Solomon?

Listen Lovey, no wassit wassit not tantarit claate nuh fi tek fi wi glory because it was not him that busted their ass off for you. I did.

You got cussing brutal for it to have this piece of crap; cesspool wuss dan di sulphur pits of earth come invade our world and space. Not a claate to yass. Man goh more than bleep yuself yu ear. This is Lovey's and my space and no degenerate of a waste chute duppy nuh fi cum roune wi.

Who di bleep do you think you are to just walse eene an tek mi prosperity and glory with Lovey soh. Burn the bleep in hell bitch; not again. You did not write these books nor did you build a good and true foundation with Lovey; I did. Lovey built good and true with me and I will not have you take what's rightfully ours; go burn in hell you bleeping demon of hell. Fuck off and leave me alone. My prosperity is not yours and I will not let you take my prosperity and glory from me. I found a good and true foundation with Lovey and I will not have you take our good and true foundation from us. You will not put your name on what I've written because I am not male, I am female thus my female name Michelle Jean. I have the name of Lovey, his earthly and spiritual name so puck you and fuck you. Dyam wrenk an outtaauda.

Lovey is the foundation of true and good life and I will not have you take Lovey's foundation either. He's worked too damn hard with me to get these books done. Glory and honour, truth and prosperity belongs to Lovey also and I refuse to have you take this from Lovey again.

<u>Look the fuck how unnu man demean him Lovey and write all kind of bullshit about him.</u> No fuck off and leave me alone because I more than infinitely and indefinitely more than forever ever condemn and curse you for this. In the name of Lovey I curse you, curse you, curse you. I lock your thieving ass in the fire pits of hell more than indefinitely.

Be gone you demon duppy from hell. Condemnation is yours thus I truly condemn you to hell; lock you in hell and destroy the key. Stay in hell because you cannot come on and will never come out because as your jail term expires so must you indefinitely.

Coo pan di book of Solomon. A fucking woman wrote that book to tell of her love; true love of Solomon an unnu black man lie bout a Solomon wrote that book when it was a woman. Fuck the lots of you, none of you will or can steal my glory ever again. Nuh mek mi tell unnu bout unnu mumma wassit wassit not tantarit claate. Check your dyam self because unnu a fucking wreck. WHA MAN EVER DU FI LOVEY?

WHA MAN DU?

All unnu du a lie an scheme and plot with the debil against him. Unnu sey unnu love but yet don't know the true mean of truth; true love.

Mi nuh write fi unnu, mi write fi Lovey and tell of my good and true truth of Lovey to the wurl. So who yu bi fi come eeene now an tek Lovey glory from mi an him?

Man goh suckout wey yu nuffi suck out you hear.
Damn bright an outta aauda.
Wey yu du fi mi an Lovey?

Not one a unnu heva help mi inna di spiritual realm. Unnu lef mi alone to solve and fix things and at the appointed hour when mi and Lovey fi live well and good and bask in our goodness; glory, yu waane cum tek wi glory from wi. Kibba yuself an tek presipit. Chuck bitch. No nigga bitches allowed. Fuck you, fuck ya, fuck ya.

An Lovey, yu ha di gaul fi mek di man; damn jackass black man cum du dis.

You truly nuh love mi do you.

Look at the legacy of you as written by men and fi wi good up good up legacy wey mi a build fi us yu a goh mek dis demon duppy tek from wi suh?

Yu really nuh noa mi eee!!

Yu noa mi Lovey?

No, yu really nuh noa mi. Thus Shelly Thunder sey, "sometimes a man fi get cuff fi get cuff." Truss mi, if it wasn't a true sin and disrespect fi cuff yu, a woulda cuff yu. No, mi nah hide an chat.

How di hell yu a goh mek disya crebbay crebbay man ya cum tek wey wi haade haade wuk soh?

A man yu prefa?

A dutty thiefing man yu prefa?

No a mus dem because yu a gi dem access fi tek wey wey wi ha an call it dem own.

Let me ask you something, a man created this universe?

Are all your children not females? So tell me, what the hell did man build a part from war machines; death?

Can a man create life if he's got no life?

Can a man be good if he's got no good will?

Remember you did show me Will and Will was a ugly male that looked like Will Smith of the physical realm.

So truly don't with me because I am truly not having it.

<u>Why the hell should a man take credit for what he did not do?</u>

This man did not clean the mess I did, so why the hell is he taking credit for what I did. I am a black woman not a black man; thus no one should take credit for what they have not done; created or invented. All too often we as women are robbed of our glory but not this one; not anymore.

As your daughter I forbid and make it sinful and condemnation of sin; curse for anyone living or dead to take credit for what they have not invented, built or build, written; write or sing. Yes artists feed off artists but the practice stops now. It must stop.

Yes it stops with me too. Thus no one can say the pictures in these are ours Lovey. These pictures are truly not ours and I will not take credit for what is truly not mine. Like I've said and will forever state and say including imply in spirit. The pictures in these books, the Michelle Jean Series of Books and the Michelle J. Lyons series of books do not belong to me; us Lovey. **_THEY ARE USED FOR ILLUSTRATION PURPOSES AND ILLUSTRATION PURPOSES ONLY._** Thus every artist's picture, song or words that is used in these books; **_I GIVE TRUE AND REAL CREDIT TO. IT'S THEIR WORK AND THEY DESERVE THE RECOGNITION AND CREDIT AND THIS RECOGNITION AND CREDIT IS TRULY GIVEN._** It was always my intention that if people liked these pictures, songs or words for you my readers, people and fam to purchase these works; support these artist for their work and efforts because their work and songs do carry weight; have a meaning. If it did not, I would not use them or give the songs and teachings in some of these books.

You did not give me a specific artist to go to Lovey; so I did my best in pictures, music and words to deliver the message and messages you want and needed to be delivered.

I know I cannot and will not stand surety for these artists; people because I truly do not know them nor do I know their content of character except for one or two. And even with me knowing the one or two, I truly cannot stand surety for them.

Michelle

Ah Lovey sometimes when you think you have friends they turn out to be false. They are the ones to screw you and sell you out to the highest bidder. You become their sacrifice here on earth.

Wow

Thus I have to ask again Lovey, is this; the filthy and nasty stories of lies and deceit that men has written about you, the legacy you want for yourself?

It's amazing how man rob and deceit and now to see them robbing me again and you've truly done nothing about it. It's as if you truly don't care about my well being and the well being of me and you.

Why should anyone rob me including you?

Why do you refuse to stop this?
Why do you continue to let man rob me and you?

Are you that powerless and blind to see and do?

<u>*This is our future Lovey, so why are you allowing filthy beasts to rob us of our wealth and dignity?*</u>

Look at what nasty beasts have and has done to you.
THEY ROBBED YOU OF YOUR GOOD AND TRUE PEOPLE.

THEY ROBBED YOU OF YOUR DIGNITY.
THEY ROBBED YOU OF YOUR HOME WITH US.

THEY ROBBED YOU OF THIS EARTH AND UNIVERSE. MADE IT SO UNCLEAN THAT YOU CANNOT LIVE IN THEM; YOU HAD TO FLEE FROM THEM.

THEY ROBBED YOU OF YOUR WATERWAYS HERE ON EARTH.

THEY ROB EARTH OF HER DIGNITY AND SELF RESPECT.

THEY ENSLAVE AND ROB YOUR PEOPLE.
THEY RAPE AND KILLS US.
ENSLAVE US.

CALL US NASTY AND FILTHY NAMES.

THEY ROBBED US OF YOUR LANGUAGE.
THEY ROBBED US OF OUR MORALS AND PRIDE; SELF RESPECT.

THEY ROBBED US OF OUR VIBRATION; CONNECTIONS WITH YOU.

THEY SHACKEL AND CHAIN US.
THEY TEACH US LIES.
TEACH US TO ACCEPT THEIR LIES AND DECEIT AND IF WE DO NOT ACCEPT THEIR LIES AND DECEIT WE ARE KILLED.

THEY TELL US, IF WE DO NOT ACCEPT GOD WE CANNOT GO TO HEAVEN.

THEY TELL US JESUS IS YOUR SON AND HE DIED FOR OUR SINS SO THAT WE CAN BE SAVED.

THEY TELL US WE HAVE TO BE BAPTIZED.
WE HAVE TO BE WASHED IN THE BLOOD.

Much more they've done to us and tell us Lovey and you're telling me you're okay with this!!!

Look at what humans have done to you. They wrote books of lies and deceit and gave it to us humans and say these filthy and nasty books of whoredom and condemnation; sin, is of you.

How do you as Lovey and God live with yourself knowing that human males and females including children have and has done this to you? Humans globally believe in this shit; the crap of shit these men women and children give us to believe in.

Now to have this; me being robbed again by my own black male. **Lovey, please do not let me go off again because I will not have anyone robbing me again. If you want humans to continue to rob you, then so be it, but truly not me.** I've battled with you fierce and hard for justice and truth for you to show mi dis stinking dutty crebbay crebbay demon a rob mi of my due speaks volumes to me when it comes to you and me. You would rather watch me suffer and feel pain rather than sey, my daughter, you want to take away my daughter's prosperity yet again? Hell no. Shi crass, temperamental, miserable, strong in words and truth; shi a sleeping lion an mi fi guh wake har fi feel her wrath? Hell no. I am stopping you because I can't take di baddaracion and ninggy ninggy inna mi ears when shi goh off.

Shi terrible inna di cussing an mi fi goh have har cuss mi reckless an rude again!!!

No, you cannot rob my child; daughter because she is not robbing you. She is just and fair and I cannot let injustice in her life anymore. In all that she has done, she did try not just for me, but for our good and true trying people; the earth and universe, the waterways, plants and trees. No you cannot hurt her again.

When you take from her unjustly you are taking from me unjustly. She did give freely in her books but this robbery I will not stand or take. She is the one to be trying to rid and clean the earth of all the filth humanity has and have left behind. She's the one to wash the feces; filth away and you are not going to take her glory by robbing her of her good and true due. I as God know fairness and she Michelle is just and fair even though shi rude and fierce; terrible inna di cussing.

Mi haffi goh wash har mouth out with soap and wash these books of her brutal cussing words, but she's mine; my great and true defender. In all she's done, she's thought about me no matter how it hurt her. She has always come to me in truth and I respect that about her; so no I will not let you hurt her anymore.

She shares with me and she's never been stingy with me. Shi greedy yes, but I truly love it when she's greedy for my true love. She's not greedy for my wealth, strength and power; she's greedy for my true love. Yes she wants stability in her life and who wouldn't given what she's faced. She's faced hell and she's still standing. Her good and true thought of me; no human being on the face of the planet Earth has ever thought of me in that way.

None have been truthful to me.

Men write but men lambaste me, treat me like shit; feces. Man put me on the same nasty level as them. So no, I cannot hurt her like this again. No man woman or child including beast and spirit, this earth and universe is allowed to rob her. Anyone rob her or harm her in anyway will more than feel my wrath and pain because I will take out my destructive anger on every human being on earth including the universe and worlds and universe you as humans don't know. Her hurt and pain stops now.

My hurt and pain stops now.

I can no longer condone anyone to hurt her or take away her prosperity. Thus let it be known globally and universally and in the spiritual realm that anyone rob her of her wealth, health, prosperity, place with me, her riches, money, joy and happiness; I will curse more than infinitely and indefinitely without end for more than indefinite generations and more than infinite and indefinite lifetimes without end.

Every human being on earth, in the spiritual realm, under the earth, above the earth, in and under the universe including the heavens and where humans reside in other worlds and universes that you on earth know not about now have my truth and worth; words of truth and true love toward my child; daughter. Just as she truly loves me more than universally and unconditionally, I more than truly love her more than universally and unconditionally.

Ah Lovey, could this be the truth and true you towards me. Ah Lovey could this be truly?

Ah Lovey, could this truly be.
Could this truly be?

Ah Lovey, you know my children take my stuff and samfy thus let them be excluded from this writ that you have between me you and humanity; the thieves and wicked of humanity. Remember I use to take my mother's things when I was younger Lovey. So truly exclude my children, but all others like di man in my dream and the man that took the sword of death from me, let them truly suffer; be cursed because it was

MY GOOD AND TRUE WILL AND I NEED

wilfully done on their part. I need prosperity Lovey and I can't have my own or any other nation take my prosperity from me. When they do this, they are taking from you too Lovey thus leaving me to argue and quarrel with you brutal.

And people what I give is truly what I give. Please do not be afraid to look into the formula and or combination I've given you in another book to help people with diabetes. This was freely given. What I am talking about and what I wrote in terms of what I would like Lovey to do has nothing to do with what I give in truth and freely.

In the spiritual realm I am being robbed of my prosperity and this isn't the first time it's happening and I am tired of it. Black Males steal from me therefore, the goodness I'm to get in the physical and spiritual realm I cannot get it. They (a black male) take my prosperity from me and I am putting a stoppage to it. I cannot allow this to continue to happen and I am hoping Lovey take notes and condemn this vile and evil man. This man and this man alone Lovey; he's the one I see doing this; taking my prosperity and glory, so therefore I have to condemn and curse him. I cannot curse all of humanity because of this man. It's simply not right thus I need you Lovey to stand up to him and lock his ass in hell indefinitely more than forever ever without end so that he cannot hurt me by taking away my prosperity and true glory ever again. Let no one else come and do this to me ever again Lovey. They are not just robbing me; they are robbing you too.

When this man do this he's taking away from my life, your life and Lovey's life; good life all around. So yes I curse him, curse him, curse him; this man in the spiritual realm and sentence him to hell where he belongs. Let him rot and burn in hell infinitely. I do not take from you so don't bleeping take from me.

Why the hell do I have to suffer financially and emotionally because of a creep like you?

No bleep off and get the bleep out of my way.

I curse you I curse you I curse you. In the name of Lovey, Good God and Allelujah; I curse you and strip you of your powers; reach here on earth. I refuse you and refuse you from taking my prosperity and Lovey's prosperity from us.

Leave us the hell alone. Stay in hell because you are bleeping hell come on now.

No Lovey fair is fair.

If men had wanted truth for self, would they not live good and true; clean?

Am I deserving of any of the hurt and pain this man is unleashing on me and my family?

Are you deserving of any of it Lovey; the hurt and pain I unleash on you? Come on now. Therefore, I've seen the evil and ugly Will of man and it's not pretty; clean. I also know the Will of man and how polluted and nasty; disgusting this will is. This is why men wrote the nasty book; their holy bible of whoredom and nastiness; condemnation of sin and sins. They are nasty and condemned; thus they want humanity to be condemned like them, hence she (the white woman) cursed the white male. And now I curse him (a black male) for taking my prosperity and glory. **<u>Thus I more than over stand and comprehend why humans have sex changes; men changing their sex to female and female changing their sex to male. They change their birth certificates also so that they can say; see world, men can have babies too. Daddy gave birth to you. So the lies and deceit; distortion of the truth by males and yes some female will never stop.</u>**

WHO THE HELL NEED TRUE FEMALES ANYMORE?

MEN ARE FEMALES AND FEMALES ARE MALES.

Not one of us can see the truth of what's going on. So, real humans won't be needed; thus synthetic beings will be the norm here on earth real soon if the wicked and evil has their own devilish and evil way.

Thus Lovey did not put enmity between his seed and the devil's seed. Men put enmity between Lovey's seed and them. Men are the driving forces behind evil and not one of us can see this. Thus it is forbidden for clean to lay with and procreate with the wicked and evil seeds of men and women; the unclean.

Go ahead and say it. Say I am bashing men and I am a male basher. I bash no one. I see the truth and speak the truth and if you don't like it too fucking bad.

WHO THE FUCK WROTE THE BIBLE?

WHO'S CAUSING ENMITY BETWEEN YOU AND GOD; THE GOD YOU CLAIM TO LOVE?

Go ahead and say it about me so I can cuss you reckless and rude.

Lovey has never denied anyone entry to his kingdom and abode. We are the ones to lock our self out.

We sinned; thus we locked our self out of his kingdom and abode. We can't get back in due to the lies and deceit, lies and deceit of self and others.

We allow men women and children to teach us and preach to us about these lies and deceit and we believe them. **WE DO NOT GO TO LOVEY AND SAY LOVEY, A TRUE WEY DI MAN SEY?**

LOVEY, EEE SEY "THOU SHALT NOT KILL," SO IF WE ARE NOT TO KILL, WHY DO POLITICIANS SEND PEOPLE ON THE BATTLEFIELD TO KILL?

LOVEY, IF WHOREDOM IS A SIN, WHY DO SOME MEN MARRY MORE THAN ONE WOMAN?

WHY ARE CHILD MARRIAGES CONDONED?

WHY ARE YOUNG CHILDREN BEING MOLESTED BY GROWN ASS MEN INCLUDING WOMEN THAT SAY THEY REPRESENT YOU?

LOVEY, IS THIS TRULY YOU?

IF YOU WERE TRUE AND CLEAN, THE TRUE AND LIVING GOD, WHY WOULD YOU PROCREATE WITH A HUMAN FEMALE TO GET JESUS?

YOU CREATED ADAM AND EVE FROM SCRATCH WITHOUT THE USE OF A SPERM AND A EGG. WHY WOULD YOU LAY WITH A WOMAN TO GET A HUMAN CHILD WHEN ALL YOU COULD HAVE DONE IS CREATE ANOTHER ONE?

Truly look into things as a person and human being. IF MEN AND NOW ALL OF HUMANITY WERE CLEAN AND TRUE; WOULD WE BE BELIEVING IN THE CRAP AND CESSPOOLS OF LIES GIVEN TO US ABOUT GOD; LOVEY?

Now, you know the truth of your biological mother and father, would you believe shit like this about them?

No right?

SO WHY BELIEVE THEM ABOUT LOVEY; GOD?

I trust Lovey to do right by me. I know his protection of me and anything I can do to help clean up the shit of man; humans, I am going to do willingly and truthfully.

I cannot let the lies told about Lovey continue, nor can I let this man continually take away my prosperity. So yes I curse and condemn him and I curse and condemn the person; whether man woman or child that caused this to happen; initiated the process. So whether male or female and it matters not the realm they are in or if they are living or dead; that person is cursed and condemned indefinitely without end.

Ah Lovey you're the greatest.

Happy holiday. Our days are on their way.

What are you going to do for my day of birth and your special day?

Lovey, are we going to walk hand in hand and truly have fun by taking a good and true vacation in 2016?

Lovey, are these books going to be our true blessings now and begin to sell so that I can give you your mega mansion of goodness and truth clean?

Lovey, are we there yet?

Are we home?

No, we are truly not home. I have not come to the end of my journey with you so that we can truly take a rest and come and or go again.

Ah Lovey.

I remember you Lovey.
I also remembered my mother.

Do you like your card Lovey?

Hopefully I can do this each and every year for you. Give you a card and flowers; just you and my mother the week before the festivities of Christmas starts.

Ah Lovey I miss you and her (my mother) I truly do. If only things were different here and I could see the both of you face to face.

Yes I am longing and it hurts that you are not here in person beside me.

It hurts that I can't rest my head on your shoulder and tell you all my troubles and pain. Yes I have these books but it's not the same as being beside you and you drying my tears. I miss her (my mom) and you so much. Why did the both of you have to go away from me in the physical?

Why do I have to yearn the both of you so much at times?

Ah Lovey, you and I know the reason but in truth, I am still hurt because none of this had to be.

We did not have to leave each other.

You could have shielded the earth from all of this and let death and his people stay on their planet; hell. Look at it, there are obstacles in our way, my way and your way Lovey. I am not sure if I can fix them all so that we can begin to clean up earth for you to come home.

I know one day which is tomorrow, but does it have to be so long for me and you and mommy; my mother Miss Peggy; Rosalind? Ah she was and still is a rose; our good and true rose. Lovey you are our root and water that make us grow in a good and true way.

Aye, you are both cherished and truly thank you both for being a part of my good and true life. And yes, although I cannot see the both of you face to face; I know you are both with me here on earth.

Michelle

MY GOOD AND TRUE WILL AND I NEED

It's December 20, 2015 and I guess in some way I know this day would come for me. But before I get into my true good will and true truth Lovey I have to ask why?

Why did you not lock this demon in hell and destroy the key like I told you to long ago?

He tied me to him and I thought I pulled his tie and all were fine with me and you Lovey?

But I guess not after my dream with him this morning. This man is still in my life creating hell for me and I need him to stop Lovey.

Why are you allowing him to take away my prosperity here on earth and in the spiritual realm?

Did you not show me him enlisting the help of other black males to harm me? So why are you prolonging this demon's spiritual life here on earth?

Why are you allowing him to steal my prosperity here on earth and in the universe and spiritual realm?

He's condemned; a true demon that refuses to leave me alone. So I am fully putting a stoppage to it right now. He is condemned and I condemn him to hell and curse him more than infinitely and indefinitely forever ever without end. I lock him in hell more than indefinitely thus none; absolutely no one on earth or in the spiritual realm can save him. He's death like his father Satan.

His mark is the inverted cross of death and you and I know this Lovey. He was and still is the downward cross that was put on earth to kill me. I know this now and I've said this in another book. I know the truth of him thus I argue with you about the way you teach us. So no, I will not save him and none of my children that I have with him here on earth can save him. It is not permissible for any of them to do. He did try to kill me in the physical and spiritual realm. So Lovey, truly let this be the end of him and me. Just as how you protect and shield as well as lock out all facets of evil from reaching your good and true people in the spiritual realm; do so for me with this man. Let all the evils that he's done to me find him and haunt him.

I truly do not fear him and I don't know why you would show me my spirit in fear. He use to haunt me and let me live in fear both spiritually and physically, but no more. Lovey, why the hell did you not let me fight him in the spiritual realm and beat the crap out of him?

Yes I know; I cannot fight, my grandmother instilled that in us; thus we do not go around fighting people, nor do we make war and strife with them; others. We are truly peaceful. But trust me, if it wasn't for the instillation of goodness; I would have beaten him like a bitch, just like boxers do their opponents. Trust me Lovey, I would have locked him so severely in hell that Satan literally cry for him and the demons of hell quake and shake in terror. Thus you know the brutally of my temper when provoked. Thus yes thank you granny for instilling goodness in me.

So Lovey, let him stay in hell and keep him there. I condemn him and curse him for more than life without end. It is that serious with me and you and you know this. Thus my anger is not getting the best of me.

Lovey he did all to destroy and kill me but you saved me. Plus you have the unedited book BEHIND THE SCARS that show what this cesspool of stench and sin did to me. I cannot edit this book because I truly cannot bear to look upon it. I went through hell because of him.

I cursed you for you to kill me because of him and you want me to save him? Never!!!!!!!!!!!!

I became bitter and vile because of him.

He turned my children against me in the living Lovey.

You see and know the struggles I face with raising the children I had with him. So yes, I forgive my children because I know the truth, but I will never ever forgive him. You have my word of truth on this come on now. So why are you permitting him to taunt me in his final hours before he goes to hell and burn? Don't let him reach out to me man come on now. You are my true love; so stay my good and true love. Don't smile Lovey because I am truly upset. I have you and have your back and you can't have mine. Come on now Lovey be fair.

Yes I've told you of my regret in not dedicating and devoting my children to you and your good and true service. I cannot go back in the past and change things, I just have to teach them true and hope they will learn one day. I also told you, no one from my lifeline otherwise called bloodline here on earth must walk in the way of evil. Every child that share my DNA and Lifeline must be honest, good, clean, truly peaceful, kind and clingy to you. They must be smart and wise, intelligent and truly truthful at all time. They cannot walk in the way of the wicked, nor can they commune with the wicked.

They must be truly just and fair and do all that is good and true for the betterment of you Lovey, the good and true people around them and the environment.

They must have good and true, harmonious and clean thoughts for self, the universe, you, this earth and the people around them.

They must be truly loving and warm as well as good in their giving. Their giving cannot be unclean, it must be clean and good; honest at all time.

They cannot have impure or negative thoughts, nor can they carry the dirty blood and dirty will of Sin.

They must be void of all that is evil and sinful; thus they must be totally pure and clean. So yes I condemn and curse him from generation to generation without end forevermore.

As for my children; please do not let this curse fall upon them or let them save him.

Lovey, I am no exception to the rule nor are my children no matter how much I truly love them. You know my good and true will of them, but I am not like Noah as told in man's nasty book.

<u>If my children cannot be saved due to sin then so be it; let thy good and true will be done. I refuse evil and I will not save evil not even if evil is my children. I tried my best to teach them right, even gave them and or dedicated a book to them and none has read it to my knowledge. My children do not listen nor do they see the good I am trying do for them so that they too can be saved. They want to find out life on their own and I have to truly let them and hope that they find a good and true way for self. Even me (I) Lovey, if you find that I am evil and wicked, don't let me in either. Lovey, when I say no evil and wickedness I mean absolutely none. Yes it would be nice to have exceptions, but you cannot have exceptions to the rule; well life. THE LAW STATES, "THE WAGES OF SIN IS DEATH." I cannot override this law nor do I want to. I've told you time and time again that what belongs to death belong to death; them. When you can stop male death, you cannot stop female death. She's the deadlier of the two and she's the one to take it all; land and people when pissed off.</u>

<u>So no, I cannot be an exception in all of this because I truly, truly, truly do not want anyone including death and the demons of hell to say you Lovey is unfair, you have exceptions.</u>

Yes I need you to truly love me and favour the good and truth I've done for you. But when it comes to life and going against the truth and cleanliness of life for me; I will not allow you to nor can you do this. You have to be truly just and fair in all that you do Lovey. You cannot have one set of laws for me and have another set for others. This is truly not right nor is it just. I cannot have you going against truth come on now.

True justice is truly not blind and can never be blind Lovey. Therefore, truth and cleanliness must stand upright and supreme more than forevermore. I truly love you and yes I will be hurt in certain things, but I cannot give wicked and evil people a home; not even if the wicked and evil people are my children and family.

So yes, I condemn him and turn his evil back on him. As for the person or persons he went to tie me and take away my life and prosperity; truly condemn and curse them for more than life forevermore. Truly lock them in hell Lovey and let them truly suffer worse than me.

Have no mercy for them for what they did to me. Thus I curse and condemn every wicked and evil voodoo priest and priestess, every wicked and evil obeah man and woman, shaman, witch, warlock, evil and wicked science man and woman that work science as known by Jamaicans and some in the world, every enchanter that go to the graves of people to wuk guzu; obeah and or evil. All their evils must be turned back on them and it matters not if they are living or dead Lovey. They take money and hurt people for profit; monetary gain. Thus I ask you, what right have they to do so?

What right have you Lovey to allow these wicked and evil people to do so?

I felt the pain of this nastiness and I am still feeling the pain of this man's nastiness.

You felt the pain of this man's nastiness too Lovey because I did take out all my anger and frustration on you. I beat you up so bad that it's a wonder you did not condemn and sin me; kuff and or beat me literally.

Thus make it truly forbidden and unlawful; sinful for clean people to marry, lie with and procreate with wicked and evil; unclean people.

I've asked you to separate good from evil here on earth just like you've done in the spiritual world Lovey. So truly begin to do this Lovey more than infinitely and indefinitely and forever ever without end. Lovey, do this, separate this man from me as you've separated good from evil in the spiritual realm. Don't let him bother me or my children ever again. So truly separate my children from him also, just like you've done in the spiritual realm with good and evil.

Now I am going to interrupt this book again.

It's December 26, 2015 and this morning my dream world was fantastic. I dreamt the darkness and or blackness; thing in me I vomited it out. Lovey that thing inside of me came out. It was black like charcoal. It came out Lovey now let me truly live and be free.

I also dream my children's father again.

Lovey what do you not get?

He's condemned to hell and you are allowing him to reach me like this again Lovey?

<u>**Lovey; why can't I rid this demon from my life?**</u>

<u>**Are demons this hard to get rid of when they stick to you in the living and in death?**</u>

His time in hell starts soon I know this. So why are you allowing him to use this child to get to me? I am not sure of this child nor does this child resemble him. Thank you for that because it's not a double standard.

LOVEY, HE'S USING THIS CHILD TO GET TO ME. Why?

In the dream; I was not sure of this baby, just like I am not sure of this baby in the living. Yes I am doing what I can given my financial and health situation. I know it's not a lot or enough, but I am trying. When you make a good and true way for me, all will be different you know this and providing this child belong to us.

So like I said, in the dream he was using this child as a pawn. He wanted me to see him in this child but I could not. Yes I was holding the child and the child, little light skinned boy of 4 months and 2 days said to me; <u>*"forgive me."*</u> I was baffled; confused.

What do I have to forgive this baby for?

This child has done me nothing. This evil demon; man has and have done me all that is wicked and evil.

It's not this child that needs forgiveness; it's him, my children's father that need forgiveness so that he can live; be saved from hell. <u>*Thus the wicked in the living and in death cries out and or cry out to the living for a saving grace.*</u>

I did not tell the child I forgive him because there was nothing to forgive this child for.

And like I said to you Lovey; <u>**"I WILL NEVER EVER FORGIVE HIM FOR WHAT HE HAS DONE TO ME."**</u>

I cannot forgive him for what he's done to you and my children either Lovey. So no matter the stunts he pulls by using this child as his pawn, it won't work. **_NO FORGIVENESS EVER PERIOD._**

Lovey, every door, window, family member, child, demon, beast, tree, waterway, land; everything that is open to him in the living and in death; spiritual realm, his side of the spiritual realm including all that I've not mentioned must be closed off from and to him just like evil is closed off in the spiritual realm from good. No exceptions Lovey. I will not save him nor will I save wicked and evil demons; people that go out of their way to hurt another human being. I did him nothing, but he did all in the living and in death; spiritual realm to kill me; take my life.

Lovey, I give no one that willingly, knowingly and purposely go out of their way to hurt another human being, You, this earth and universe, animals and trees, the waterway and food of life a saving grace. They are more than infinitely and indefinitely more than forever ever without end locked out of our kingdom and abode just like evil is locked away from the good and true spirits of the spiritual realm and universe. Absolutely no entry must be given Lovey; so please truly keep my good and true will with you always.

So no dictator.
Lovey I know this banning more than infinitely and indefinitely belong to you. But absolutely no clergy

member; pope, imam, sheik, pastor, deacon, deaconess, priest, rabbi, elder, wicked and evil parishioner and so forth are allowed under any circumstances.

Absolutely no evil and wicked politician
No wicked and evil human being
Wicked and evil animals
Wicked and evil beasts

<u>Absolutely no skin bleacher. You've accepted spiritual death in the living so you truly cannot be saved.</u>

No tattooed freaks of any kind. Tattoos are of death; the gangs of death, thus absolutely no gang member period.

Absolutely no lodge man woman or child of any kind. So if you are affiliated with the order of death (Illuminati, Free Mason, Shriners, DeLawrence and or DeLaurence, Scientology and what have you) to name a few, you are more than infinitely and indefinitely locked out just like the evil spirits are locked out of the realm of good people in the spiritual realm. You accepted death in the living thus condemning your children, family and friends to death. Some of you make sacrifices unto death thus killing family members, friends, and colleagues. Some of you drink blood and urine; bathe in blood and urine; eat human flesh and feces and more. All you do, you do for death and the reward of death; thus locking yourself out of life. You condemned your own children to death; thus your hate of your own children is truly beyond me literally.

Absolutely no Babylonian is allowed. Their god is truly not you Lovey. I cannot give them entry nor will I lift their indefinite ban. Their ban stays. I cannot undo nor will I undo what another messenger has and have done long before me.

No Nigerian, German or South African White will I save.

Nigerian due to what that scum group Boko Haram has and have done to the people of Nigeria for death and so much more.

Germans due to the burning of the Jamaican Flag of life and me taking my anger and frustration out on Lovey and he told me yet again to write a book. Yes Germans have and has done a lot more atrocities to people. They've massacred in the name of Germany; supremacy. Just look at what they did to the natives of Namibia.

White South Africans because of what they did to Tata Madiba; Nelson Mandela and so much more. (The treatment of Black People in their own land). 27 years did they lock him away for wanting what's best for his people. So because of this and more, I give no White South African a saving grace.

Also Lovey, the curse that the white woman put on the White Man and or White Race truly stays. I will not lift this ban because in all you see and know here on earth; it's the White Race that did the majority of the damage. So no, this curse stays. I've seen too much and read too much to lift this curse. So these people must stay locked out more than infinitely and indefinitely just like how the wicked and evil spirits and or beings are locked out from the good of the spiritual realm.

Transgender it things. Under no circumstances....no they have no chance in hell to be saved period. Thus they are truly locked away from humanity in both worlds; the physical and spiritual. They are more than a condemnation of sin because they pollute everywhere they go. So this condemnation and ban; more than indefinite lock out stays period. Nothing can or will save them if there is a saving grace for all.

As for the wicked and evil of my homeland; land of birth, you have absolutely no saving grace period. You are locked out just like the wicked and evil are locked out of the spiritual realm from the good people and spirits of that realm.

Wicked and evil everything and anything including all I've not mentioned must not be given a saving grace Lovey. I will not save them. I will however lock them out just like the wicked and evil is locked away from the good people and beings; spirits of the spiritual realm, and I've truly done this Lovey.

Absolutely no wicked and evil can use a child to convey their evil message and or messages to anyone every again Lovey. So truly let all evil be fully and truly over.

Lovey, evil cannot change and I've told you this in another book. Evil seek to destroy and kill and this is what evil people has and have done here on earth.

Look at what evil men wrote about you and gave to humanity and say it is holy.

They taught us their evil ways; now billions follow these wicked and unclean people to their deaths; hell.

You know the fairness of life Lovey; thus you have to be fair and just. You cannot be weak and I won't let you.

Life isn't about weakness; thus shield and protect us from these wicked and evil people including wicked and evil spirits; demons. You see how my spirit cry out to you not to be in their company or have them (the wicked and evil) come into my home and domain with you. So let good start repelling evil Lovey. Let us start separating self from them so that we can truly start cleaning up self for the better come on now.

Wicked and evil people see no wrong in what they do Lovey. You and I including others are a testament of this. Evil think all they do is good; so tell me what good can come from true evil?

Remember he turned my children against me. I did all in goodness and in truth to help him and he assonated my character, told lies against me, did all to hurt and kill me here in the living and in death; spiritual realm. **_SO EVIL CANNOT CHANGE IN THE LIVING AND EVIL CANNOT CHANGE IN THE SPIRITUAL REALM. SO FOR HIM LOVEY, NO ACCESS; ACCESS IS MORE THAN TRULY AND INDEFINITELY DENIED._**

Good cannot live in peace or true peace whilst evil is around. You and I know this Lovey. So why are you keeping good and true people amongst the wicked and evil?

Nothing good can come from true evil Lovey.

Evil and wicked people render evil and wickedness on all those who are trying to help them. **_You are no exception Lovey come on now._**

Look at how you've tried to help us as humans. Have humans not render evil onto you for all the good you've done to and for us?

No, don't turn away and cry Lovey. You tired your best to help us, and look at the garbage and nastiness we believe when it comes to you.

Look at the death toll and sins here on earth and in the universe. Look at the killings humans do here on earth and in the universe. Tell me, is any of this killing; death warranted?

Look at how we hate and enslave each other.

Look at how we rape each other including Mother Earth.

Look at how we rape you and take good life from you Lovey. So tell me if I am the only one who feels the hurt and pain of wicked and evil people?

Do you not feel this hurt and pain Lovey?

You feel it and know it. So no, I refuse to save wicked and evil people including my own. Thus I tell you, only family members who are dear to me will I save and it's not many that I will save. I truly do not know all of my family from both sides; mother and father. I stay away from people; thus I stay away from family too and you know this. They (my family) know this too.

You are my tool and refuge Lovey.

Why would I refuse and condemn you and the good you've done for me? I cannot do this, nor will I do it. Thus I know the truth in you. I value our morals and truth; so why would I give away the life and truth you've given me for or to the wicked and evil?

It's not render evil unto me and I give you goodness in return. I will not give evil any goodness because I've learnt the hard way that when you give evil goodness, you are giving away your good up good up life and goodness; prosperity. When you do this, you are condemned like the wicked and evil. Your goodness you can never ever get back no matter how hard you try. I am a living testament of this Lovey.

Look how hard I've been trying with you for goodness; true goodness and truth and it's not forth coming the way I want and need it to come. Sometimes I am hungry and in need and it's you that I have to cry out to for help.

Look at my health and financial woes; my health and financial debt load.

I'm not the only one that this is happening to Lovey come on now.

No Lovey, I cannot with evil and wicked people anymore. You mean too much to me for me to disappoint you. So no, my children and I are no exception to the rule; your law and laws of life. None, not one of us can live unfair and expect to get fair; be fair in life come on now.

Look at how you gave my homeland your name and life.

Look at how you gave the United States of America your good up good up spiritual life and they destroyed you.

America spend billions of dollars; over 700 billion dollars each year on death alone whilst their children and people go hungry living in the streets.

Look at how they America; Americans promote death for death. All that is nasty, wicked and evil they sell on the behalf of death for death.

None realize that death can only give death; death cannot give life and all that death give you is only temporary. Must be given back to death in slavery; death. America claim to be a superpower. But what country that is a superpower is indebted to death?

What superpower leaves their children and people living and dying in the streets for the basic necessities of life; needs and wants? Come on now.

What superpower has a debt load in the trillions monetary? Trillions of dollars neither land and people can repay. So yes, Israel and Judah whored and now both lands must pay. So as I take the flag of life of Jamaica and give it back to you Lovey and you handed it back to me, and because of our Royal Lifeline and because I know it is not wrong to take back your eye in the upright triangle; I now take spiritual life, the eye in the upright triangle from the United States of America indefinitely and hand it back to you for good and safe keeping. **<u>Death must not have life.</u>** *Death claimed this land and no matter the ordinance, Death owns America; thus this land cannot be saved. The debts and or sins of America; Americans in America and globally, no one can truly repay and you know this Lovey. So as your good and true life was taken from Jamaica, Egypt, Ethiopia, Nigeria and some European lands, I now take final life,* physical and spiritual life from the land of America; the United States of America forevermore. This is the land of the damned because they promote death of every kind on every level of life where life exist.

Their monetary note must now be reduced to naught and they can no longer use the eye in the upright triangle on anything. It is now forbidden, thus death failed; cannot have their NEW WORLD ORDER OF DEATH. Thus the eye in the upright triangle must be a true curse unto those that use it falsely.

DEATH FALSIFY LIFE NOT LIFE FALSIFY DEATH.

LIFE IS CLEAN AND CAN NEVER BE FALSE OR DIRTY. THUS THE WAGES OF SIN IS DEATH BECAUSE YOU'VE BECOME DEAD AND OR LIKE UNTO THE DEAD.

Life must live on and walk on in truth; true peace and cleanliness; harmony.

Goodness begets goodness Lovey and this land is truly not good. They design to destroy and kill.

They promote immorality; sins all around.

They condemned many lands on earth including their own. Now just as my homeland have to pay for their sins for going against truth; the law and laws of truth, so must America; modern day Israel also.

Truly take back and keep life Lovey because as humans we are truly not deserving of you; nor are we deserving of life. We destroy and kill life instead of preserving and cherishing life.

So now you know and have my good and true will Lovey. Yes I am truly sorry I could not give you all good and true because you are deserving of it. I cannot be unjust or unfair because I too have sinned against you despite you asking me to write you a book. So yes give evil back dem dutty bloody wata. Gi dem back dem dutty blood wey dem lef inna wi good up good up human body and or flesh.

Gi dem bak dem dead God and world; Hell.

Gi dem bak dem evil and nasty everything Lovey.
We truly don't need it Lovey.

We need your good and true clean wata and life. Good over evil at all time and truly thank you for making me so fierce. So protection protection is what I truly need.

Michelle

Look into things and all that I've written for you.

Lovey as this is my good and true will, please let no more evil spirit torment little babies or anyone for that matter ever again or anymore.

Let no evil spirit wait in the wings to possess them or anyone either.

And please truly put a stoppage to people coming to my home unannounced. I truly do not care who it is. They cannot just show up at my doorstep.

Let my children put a stoppage to this nonsense also. I need my privacy and I have to live private. I do not want to be a part of social media where you have to publicise your life and body to the world. What happens in my home stays in my home. What you want me to write and tell the world this remain the same Lovey. But as for my private life that you give me with someone it must be extremely private and guarded.

My personal life with my children must be totally private. We must live privately and away from social media and the spotlight. We will be truly giving, but personally we have to be private and devoted to you Lovey. No scandal must we have and we must not be scandalous. Peaceful, truly peaceful must we be; thus we must not live for strife, nor can we put enmity and strife between anyone. I do not teach my children to fight or pick up arms and it's going to stay this way indefinitely. True peace must we carry and truly peaceful must we be. We cannot deviate from this nor can we be like those that cry peace but yet war with you and kill you.

You are Allelujah Lovey. Some say Allah, but you are Allelujah; the Breath of Life and we are to keep the Breath of Life; You, true and pure; clean at all time. We cannot say we have life and live for death and give death come on now.

Lovey, what I truly need from you is for you to close off this earth from all facets evil spirit and people; negative forces or energy indefinitely for more than forever ever without end and I've told you this repeatedly; over and over again. Good and evil cannot cohabitate in the spiritual realm thus they (good and bad) are closed off from each other. So please do the same here on earth as you did in the spiritual realm Lovey.

<u>Lovey, once evil and wicked people pass away, truly let them be cut off from all life here on earth.</u> *Let them not be able to come back; thus void the 40 days and 40 nights that they stay on earth to create havoc. I know it's more than 40 days and forty nights they have; it's years that they have; thus void this privilege Lovey. No one needs to be around the dead in the living come on now. Once you're dead; stay the hell dead if you are wicked and evil come on now. It's been years that this man has and have been tormenting me and it has to stop. Let him be truly gone because like I said Lovey; no* saving grace I give the wicked and evil globally and universally.

No one should bring evil into this world Lovey, thus the practice of good procreating with wicked and evil people must stop indefinitely. Respect is due and we are to respect our self come on now.

<u>Good must procreate with good only. This must be law Lovey and everyone must adhere to this law. If humans cannot adhere to this law then none must be allowed to have children; they must be born barren and void of the gift of life.</u>

Lovey please please hear me and truly do; help me.

Lovey, if I am wrong in anything I write let me truly find my wrongs and errors and correct them.

Before I close this book, please help me with my dream world and visions as of 2016. Also, if it be thy will let me know how to write and read your language so that we do not have any communication problems. Our vibe and vibration must be unified and in unison Lovey come on now. I cannot write for you and obstacles be in our way come on now.

Lovey please do not let me have to decipher and or figure out my dreams anymore. Some of them are too hard and complicated.

Please let my dreams be clear and true.

No more tainted dreams where males can represent females and females represent males.

No more distortion Lovey.

No more lies.

No more confusion.

No more heartache and pain Lovey come on now.

So clear messages that are exact and void of deciphering.

So do take care.

Oh, do forgive me of the Shelly Thunder analogy with you once again. You are my truth and I so need you to truly listen to me and hear me.

Do take care of my mother; gorgeous mother as usual and you take care of yourself. I am counting on you for this.

I am going to add I Need to this book because I only have a few pages in that book. And as always, you are the final sayer in all of this. I can only come to you with my good and true desires and it's up to you to look into things and make the right fair and just decision. Yes I know I put pressure on you and I am truly sorry, but I have to.

Remember, you're my bestest of friend and I tell you everything. So come 2016, no more keeping me lonely.

No more making me cry with grief.

I need happiness so truly factor mega loads of happiness for me you and our good and true people always.

We have to travel travel travel and we must be truly healthy, emotionally and financially. We have to be stable Lovey, so no more yoyo emotions of insanity and near insanity mentally and spiritually.

And yes, I am still waiting on you for that good and true person that you've ordained for me. You know my preference; flavour, so no more undesirables; people that truly do not fit into our portfolio of cleanliness and truth.

Michelle

I NEED

In all we do, we need truth
Hope
Life
True love

In all we say, we need truth
A secure home
Good and true people to call friend

In all we see, we need truth
A good and clear; strong and clean foundation
God; Good God and Allelujah, Lovey

In all we need
We need truth
Life
Care
Security
A clean and pure heart
Hope
A good home
Lovey

Michelle

Lovey, why make us old and forgetful?

Why do we age so poorly and frail?

It's so weird that we live our lives and in old age we are forgotten. It's only when we die you see the crocodile tears from friends and loved ones professing to care; love you. They didn't remember you in the living so why are they remembering you in death?

What sense does that make?

Don't be a hypocrite. If you know not someone in the living; truly do not know them when they are dead come on now.

Lovey, why is it in death you are remembered?

Why do people cry for you and they know not you?

Why forget someone in the living and only remember them in death?

I truly don't know Lovey. I guess it's because I just talked to Pastor Wright and he could not remember me. Yes he's old and I wanted to wish him Merry Christmas and to hear him recollecting where he lived in Jamaica when he was younger got to me.

Yes I am worried about him because he was good to me and my family. I don't talk about him much because there are things in life left unsaid, therefore, I don't say them.

It's sad though that we've come so far in life to forget and yes die.

Yes I am worried about my state of mind and well being because in truth, I truly don't want to be forgetful in my old age.

Dementia is a bitch Lovey and when you are on your own like him and up there in age gets to me.

Yes I know death is upon him but what can I do?
I cannot help him because health wise I am not so sound either.

I tried reaching out to the church we went to back in the day but it's closed and it's expected; it's Christmas Day. No, I did not leave a message and yes I did see his death in the waking moments after speaking him Pastor Wright. Thus death for some is truly not pretty; it's truly ugly.

Ah Lovey, do we even think of our age; how old we get?

Yes I am truly looking forward to reaching my milestone; 50th and you know this. I am so joyful and joyous because this is a true milestone and an accomplishment for me. So yes, Happy 50th; half a century for me and you Lovey. But I am not looking forward to dementia and forgetting my true loved ones.

Lovey, am I going to forget you when I get up there in age?

Lovey, are you going to make me blind and dependent on others?

Are you going to forget me and toss me to the side like I do not matter to you anymore?

What about us and our future Lovey?

I more than need you but to forget you, are you truly going to let this happen to me?

How will I live if I forget about you?
How will I be in life?

Will I not be dead without you Lovey?

So are you going to let me have dementia Lovey?

Are you going to take you away from me?

I'm already ailing as it is already, but to lose you and forget you, I truly cannot live with Lovey.

Lovey what am I going to do without you?

Why should I be forgetful and forget about you?

Yes my heart is aching right now so truly tell me what to do?

How can I fix my health so that I truly don't forget?

I need my mind to be sharp and smart.
I need to keep my wit and fierceness of you and me.

When I lose these things Lovey, I truly have nothing because in truth, you are not with me and I am all alone; left alone. So Lovey, health wise be there for me. Help me to fix all that is broken in me and on me not just in spirit but in flesh also.

Yes I feel sorry for Pastor Wright but what can I do?

I know I am not there for my father because of lies, but I am trying. Yes I need to do more but I can only do so much. And in truth, all that I think and do, I truly have you as my earthly and spiritual father. I can't do without you because you and my mom are there for me and I have to do for the both of you truthfully and honestly.

My way is not clear without the both of you. You're both my hope and good light including thought. So why would you let me grow so old that I would forget you and mom?

MY GOOD AND TRUE WILL AND I NEED

Why would you take my truth from me in that way?

I know it's not happened yet Lovey and I pray it doesn't happen. Therefore I am coming to you right now in this way. Yes the tears are there and the aching is there, but what can I do to preserve my cognitive thoughts; the truth and true thinking of my brain? I need to think of you daily Lovey. I have to truly nag you.

I have to talk to you my way. Our communication of truth is imperative to me and in all that I do. Lovey I can't lose you, I truly can't.

Why do you want to leave me Lovey?

Am I that burdensome that you would let me forget you; all we share; do?

Ah Lovey only you know right now, only you know.

Yes I am getting weak thus truly have mercy on me and read these books. See the spelling mistakes, misspelt words; errors and truly forgive me. I could not do any better. Sometimes I did not want to edit and I didn't.

Lovey truly have mercy on my tomorrows and take charge of all my tomorrows for me in a good and true way. Be my true guiding light because I need you more than ever now. Certain things I know and I have to clarify but I cannot do them now; tonight. Tomorrow is there, so truly let tomorrow be ours in a good true and positive way. Truly be my children's true guiding light and guide the with truth always.

As for the good seeds you've given me, never let them go. Guide them good and true and never let them become forgetful in old age. Never let them lose sight physically and spiritually. Let not their bodies degenerate like mine and protect them from all health woes here on earth and in the spiritual realm. Do this also for my children Lovey because you alone know. As for me, I leave my decaying health here on earth and in the spiritual realm in your hands. I am truly hoping that you will let me find all the help I truly need to secure my body, eyes, brain, heart, liver, kidneys, pancreas, feet, hands, skin, bum bum, vagina, nose, hair, ears, teeth, tongue; all within and outside of me.

Lovey hear me today and take death from my life. Let me be free to live until it's time to join you truly.

Have mercy on you too Lovey and truly remember my mother also. I truly need the both of you right now.

Michelle
December 25 and 26, 2015

OTHER BOOKS BY MICHELLE JEAN

Blackman Redemption – The Fall of Michelle Jean
Blackman Redemption – After the Fall Apology
Blackman Redemption – World Cry – Christine Lewis
Blackman Redemption
Blackman Redemption – The Rise and Fall of Jamaica
Blackman Redemption – The War of Israel
Blackman Redemption – The Way I Speak to God
Blackman Redemption – A Little Talk With Man
Blackman Redemption – The Den of Thieves
Blackman Redemption – The Death of Jamaica
Blackman Redemption – Happy Mother's Day
Blackman Redemption – The Death of Faith
Blackman Redemption – The War of Religion
Blackman Redemption – The Death of Russia
Blackman Redemption – The Truth
Blackman Redemption – Spiritual War
Blackman Redemption – The Youths
Blackman Redemption – Black Man Where Is Your God?

The New Book of Life
The New Book of Life – A Cry For The Children
The New Book of Life – Judgement
The New Book of Life – Love Bound
The New Book of Life – Me
The New Book of Life – Life

Just One of Those Days
Book Two – Just One of Those Days
Just One of Those Days – Book Three The Way I Feel
Just One of Those Days – Book Four

The Days I Am Weak
Crazy Thoughts – My Book of Sin
Broken
Ode to Mr. Dean Fraser

A Little Little Talk
A Little Little Talk – Book Two

Prayers
My Collective
A Little Talk/A Time For Fun and Play
Simple Poems
Behind The Scars
Songs of Praise And Love

Love Bound
Love Bound – Book Two

Dedication Unto My Kids
More Talk
Saving America From A Woman's Perspective
My Collective the Other Side of Me
My Collective the Dark Side of Me
A Blessed Day
Lose To Win
My Doubtful Days – Book One

My Little Talk With God
My Little Talk With God – Book Two

A Different Mood and World – Thinking

My Nagging Day

My Nagging Day – Book Two
Friday September 13, 2013
My True Love
It Would Be You
My Day

A Little Advice – Talk
1313, 2032, 2132 – The End of Man
Tata

MICHELLE'S BOOK BLOG – BOOKS 1 – 22

My Problem Day
A Better Way
Stay – Adultery and the Weight of Sin – Cleanliness Message

Let's Talk
Lonely Days – Foundation
A Little Talk With Jamaica – As Long As I Live
Instructions For Death
My Lonely Thoughts
My Lonely Thoughts – Book Two
My Morning Talks – Prayers With God
What A Mess
My Little Book
A Little Word With You
My First Trip of 2015
Black Mother – Mama Africa
Islamic Thought
My California Trip January 2015
My True Devotion by Michelle – Michelle Jean
My Many Questions To God

My Talk
My Talk Book Two
My Talk Book Three – The Rise of Michelle Jean
My Talk Book Four
My Talk Book Five
My Talk Book Six
My Talk Book Seven
My Talk Book Eight – My Depression
My Talk Book Nine – Death
My Talk Book Ten – Wow
My Day – Book Two
My Talk Book Eleven – What About December?
Haven Hill
What About December – Book Two
My Talk Book Twelve – Summary and or Confusion
My Talk Book Thirteen
My Talk Book Fourteen – My Talk With God
My Talk Book Fifteen – My Talk
My Thoughts – Freedom
My Heart to Heart With Lovey – God

Letters to my song and words of praise and truth; My true and unconditional Love; Lovey, Good God and Allelujah

Caged
Why
I Don't Know But I Know
Our Journey/ My Anger
Real Situation
December 2015
Confusion or Confession